CCSP Exam Prep

400 Practice Questions

1st Edition

www.versatileread.com

Document Control

Proposal Name	:	CCSP Exam Prep: 400 Practice Questions
Document Edition	:	1st
Document Release Date	:	21st May 2024
Reference	:	CCSP
VR Product Code	:	20241502CCSP

Feedback:

If you have any comments regarding the quality of this book or otherwise alter it to better suit your needs, you can contact us through email at info@versatileread.com

Please make sure to include the book's title and ISBN in your message.

About the Contributors:

Nouman Ahmed Khan

AWS/Azure/GCP-Architect, CCDE, CCIEx5 (R&S, SP, Security, DC, Wireless), CISSP, CISA, CISM, CRISC, ISO27K-LA is a Solution Architect working with a global telecommunication provider. He works with enterprises, mega-projects, and service providers to help them select the best-fit technology solutions. He also works as a consultant to understand customer business processes and helps select an appropriate technology strategy to support business goals. He has more than eighteen years of experience working with global clients. One of his notable experiences was his tenure with a large managed security services provider, where he was responsible for managing the complete MSSP product portfolio. With his extensive knowledge and expertise in various areas of technology, including cloud computing, network infrastructure, security, and risk management, Nouman has become a trusted advisor for his clients.

Abubakar Saeed

Abubakar Saeed is a trailblazer in the realm of technology and innovation. With a rich professional journey spanning over twenty-nine years, Abubakar has seamlessly blended his expertise in engineering with his passion for transformative leadership. Starting humbly at the grassroots level, he has significantly contributed to pioneering the Internet in Pakistan and beyond. Abubakar's multifaceted experience encompasses managing, consulting, designing, and implementing projects, showcasing his versatility as a leader.

His exceptional skills shine in leading businesses, where he champions innovation and transformation. Abubakar stands as a testament to the power of visionary leadership, heading operations, solutions design, and integration. His emphasis on adhering to project timelines and exceeding customer expectations has set him apart as a great leader. With an unwavering commitment to adopting technology for operational simplicity and enhanced efficiency, Abubakar Saeed continues to inspire and drive change in the industry.

Dr. Fahad Abdali

Dr. Fahad Abdali is an esteemed leader with an outstanding twenty-year track record in managing diverse businesses. With a stellar educational background, including a bachelor's degree from the prestigious NED University of Engineers & Technology and a Ph.D. from the University of Karachi, Dr. Abdali epitomizes academic excellence and continuous professional growth.

Dr. Abdali's leadership journey is marked by his unwavering commitment to innovation and his astute understanding of industry dynamics. His ability to navigate intricate challenges has driven growth and nurtured organizational triumph. Driven by a passion for excellence, he stands as a beacon of inspiration within the business realm. With his remarkable leadership skills, Dr. Fahad Abdali continues to steer businesses toward unprecedented success, making him a true embodiment of a great leader.

Muniza Kamran

Muniza Kamran is a technical content developer in a professional field. She crafts clear and informative content that simplifies complex technical concepts for diverse audiences, with a passion for technology. Her expertise lies in Microsoft, cybersecurity, cloud security and emerging technologies, making her a valuable asset in the tech industry. Her dedication to quality and accuracy ensures that her writing empowers readers with valuable insights and knowledge. She has done certification in SQL database, database design, cloud solution architecture, and NDG Linux unhatched from CISCO.

Table of Contents

VERSAtile Reads

About CCSP Certification

Introduction

This chapter provides an introduction to the CCSP (Certified Cloud Security Professional) certification, highlighting its pivotal role in the domain of cloud security, risk management, and governance. It emphasizes the benefits of obtaining CCSP certification, outlines the certification process, and stresses the importance of maintaining ethical practices. Additionally, it explores the increasing need for CCSP-certified professionals in the evolving landscape of cloud security, setting the stage for further discussion on exam preparation and career paths.

What is a CCSP?

The Certified Cloud Security Professional (CCSP) is a globally recognized certification designed for professionals involved in securing cloud environments. Developed and maintained by (ISC)², the CCSP certification validates expertise in cloud security architecture, design, operations, and governance. CCSP holders demonstrate competency in addressing the unique security challenges posed by cloud computing, such as data privacy, compliance, risk management, and access control. This certification is ideal for IT and information security professionals, including enterprise architects, security administrators, systems engineers, and consultants, who are responsible for implementing and managing cloud security solutions.

Benefits of CCSP

Earning the Certified Cloud Security Professional (CCSP) certification offers numerous advantages for professionals in the cybersecurity field. Firstly, CCSP is widely recognized and respected globally, providing instant credibility and validation of expertise in cloud security. This recognition translates into enhanced career opportunities and potential advancements within one's current organization. With the ever-growing demand for cloud security expertise, CCSP-certified professionals often enjoy increased earning potential compared to their non-certified peers. Additionally, pursuing CCSP certification involves the in-depth study of cloud security principles, technologies, and best practices, expanding one's knowledge base and skill set in this critical area of IT. By obtaining CCSP certification, professionals are better equipped to mitigate risks associated with cloud computing, addressing the security challenges that accompany the adoption of cloud services.

Moreover, CCSP certification aligns individuals with market demand, positioning them as valuable assets to organizations seeking skilled cloud security professionals. Beyond career benefits, CCSP certification offers opportunities for networking, knowledge sharing, and professional growth within a global community of cloud security experts. Overall, CCSP certification serves as a pathway for professionals to elevate their expertise, advance their careers, and contribute effectively to securing cloud environments in today's digital age.

The CCSP Certification Process

The CCSP (Certified Cloud Security Professional) certification process involves several steps to demonstrate proficiency in cloud security principles and practices:

1. **Eligibility**: Before pursuing CCSP certification, candidates must meet specific eligibility requirements set by (ISC)². Typically, candidates must have a minimum of five years of cumulative, paid work experience in information technology, of which three years must be in information security and one year in one or more of the six domains of the CCSP Common Body of Knowledge (CBK).
2. **Preparation**: Once eligible, candidates undertake comprehensive study and preparation for the CCSP exam. This may involve self-study using official study materials provided by (ISC)², attending training courses, participating in study groups, or using other resources such as books and practice exams.
3. **Exam Registration**: Candidates must register for the CCSP exam through the (ISC)² website or authorized testing centers. Payment of exam fees is typically required at this stage.

4. **Exam**: The CCSP exam consists of multiple-choice questions designed to assess candidates' knowledge and understanding of cloud security concepts across six domains: Cloud Concepts, Architecture, and Design; Cloud Data Security; Cloud Platform and Infrastructure Security; Cloud Application Security; Operations; and Legal, Risk, and Compliance. The exam is timed, and candidates must achieve a passing score to earn the certification.

5. **Endorsement**: After passing the exam, candidates must complete an endorsement process where they provide proof of their professional experience and agree to the (ISC)² Code of Ethics. This endorsement is typically completed online through the (ISC)² portal.

6. **Certification**: Upon successful completion of the endorsement process, candidates officially become CCSP-certified. They receive a certificate from (ISC)² and gain access to a range of benefits, including membership in a global community of cloud security professionals, continuing education opportunities, and access to exclusive resources.

7. **Continuing Education:** CCSP certification holders are required to maintain their certification by earning Continuing Professional Education (CPE) credits and paying an annual maintenance fee. This ensures that certified professionals stay up-to-date with evolving cloud security practices and maintain their expertise over time.

Experience Requirements

The CCSP (Certified Cloud Security Professional) certification requires candidates to fulfill specific experience criteria before they can pursue the credential. To be eligible, candidates must possess a minimum of five years of cumulative, paid work experience in Information Technology (IT). Among these five years, a minimum of three years must be dedicated to information security roles, emphasizing practical experience in securing digital assets and mitigating cyber threats. Additionally, candidates must have at least one year of experience in one or more of the six domains outlined in the CCSP Common Body of Knowledge (CBK), which include Cloud Concepts, Architecture, and Design; Cloud Data Security; Cloud Platform and Infrastructure Security; Cloud Application Security; Operations; and Legal, Risk, and Compliance. This prerequisite ensures that CCSP candidates have a robust foundation in both IT and information security domains, providing

VERSAtile Reads

them with the necessary expertise to navigate the complexities of cloud security effectively.

ISACA Codes of Professional Ethics

The ISACA (Information Systems Audit and Control Association) Code of Professional Ethics serves as a foundational framework governing the conduct of ISACA members and certified professionals. Comprising four essential components, this code emphasizes the principles of individual integrity, objectivity and independence, due care and competence, and confidentiality. Firstly, it mandates the demonstration of honesty, integrity, and diligence in all professional endeavors, stressing the avoidance of conflicts of interest and the maintenance of stakeholders' trust. Secondly, it requires members and certified professionals to uphold objectivity and independence in their judgments and decisions, steering clear of circumstances that may compromise impartiality. Thirdly, it demands the exercise of due care and competence, necessitating continual learning and skill enhancement to deliver high-quality work that meets professional standards. Lastly, it emphasizes the preservation of confidentiality, mandating the protection of sensitive information from unauthorized disclosure and ensuring its use only for legitimate purposes. Adherence to this code is paramount for upholding professional integrity, fostering stakeholder trust, and advancing the profession's reputation. Violations may result in disciplinary action, highlighting the significance of ethical conduct in ISACA's community.

The Certification Exam

The CCSP (Certified Cloud Security Professional) certification exam evaluates candidates' comprehension and proficiency in cloud security management. This comprehensive assessment is designed to gauge candidates' grasp of fundamental concepts, principles, and practices pertaining to cloud security architecture, design, operations, and compliance.

The CCSP exam consists of 125 multiple-choice questions distributed across six domains as follows:

- **Cloud Concepts, Architecture, and Design:** This domain evaluates candidates' understanding of cloud computing concepts, cloud architecture principles, and cloud service models.
- **Cloud Data Security:** Candidates are assessed on their knowledge of data security issues, encryption techniques, and data lifecycle management in cloud environments.
- **Cloud Platform and Infrastructure Security:** This domain focuses on evaluating candidates' proficiency in securing cloud infrastructure, virtualization, and containerization technologies.
- **Cloud Application Security:** Candidates must demonstrate their understanding of securing cloud-based applications, including identity and access management, secure software development practices, and application security controls.
- **Operations:** This domain assesses candidates' knowledge of cloud security operations, including configuration management, monitoring, and incident response in cloud environments.
- **Legal, Risk, and Compliance:** Candidates are evaluated on their comprehension of legal and regulatory requirements, risk management principles, and compliance considerations in cloud security.

To pass the CCSP exam, candidates must exhibit a thorough understanding of these domains and associated topics, demonstrating their ability to apply cloud security best practices effectively. Achieving a passing score on the exam is a crucial milestone toward earning the CCSP certification and validating proficiency in cloud security management.

Exam Information

Certified Cloud Security Professional

Prior Certification	**Exam Validity**
No	3 Years
Exam Fee	**Exam Duration**
$599	180 Minutes
No. of Questions	**Passing Marks**
125	700/1000 points

Recommended Experience
Five years of info security experience, and 5 years of IT work.

Exam Format
Multiple Choice Questions.

Languages
English

Exam Preparation

Before Exam

To prepare for the CCSP exam, it's essential to start by thoroughly reviewing the exam content outline provided by (ISC)². This outline delineates the domains and topics that will be covered in the exam, giving you a clear roadmap of what to focus on. Once you have familiarized yourself with the content, it's time to dive into study materials. Utilize a variety of resources such as textbooks, official (ISC)² publications, online courses, and practice exams to reinforce your understanding of cloud security concepts.

Day of Exam

On exam day, it is crucial to arrive early at the exam center to allow for check-in procedures and to settle in before the exam begins. Be sure to bring along all required documents, including valid identification and any other materials specified by the exam center. Once the exam starts, maintain a calm and focused mindset. Take deep breaths to help manage any nerves, and read each question carefully to fully understand what is being asked. Avoid feeling overwhelmed by difficult questions by staying focused and maintaining confidence in your abilities. Managing your time effectively is essential during the exam. Pace yourself to ensure you have enough time to answer all questions thoroughly. If you encounter particularly challenging questions, consider flagging them for review and returning to them later if time permits. By following these tips, you will be better equipped to navigate the exam confidently and achieve success.

After Exam

After completing the exam, it is important to take time to reflect on your performance. Identify areas where you excelled and areas where there is room for improvement. If you have access to your exam results, review any questions you missed to understand why you answered incorrectly and learn from your mistakes. This reflection process helps solidify your understanding of the material and prepares you for future exams or real-world scenarios. To continue growing in cloud security expertise, stay proactive in your learning journey. Attend training sessions, workshops, and conferences to stay updated with developments in the field. These opportunities provide invaluable insights and allow you to expand your knowledge and skills.

Retaining your Certified Cloud Security Professional (CCSP)

Retaining your Certified Cloud Security Professional (CCSP) certification involves a commitment to ongoing learning and meeting maintenance requirements set by (ISC)², the certifying organization. Here's what you need to know about Continuing Education (CPE) and CPE Maintenance Fees:

Continuing Education (CPE):

Continuing Education ensures that CCSP-certified professionals stay current with the latest developments, best practices, and emerging trends in cloud security. CPE activities encompass a broad range of learning opportunities, including attending conferences, workshops, seminars, and webinars and completing training courses relevant to cloud security. Additionally, engaging in industry-related projects, self-study programs, and knowledge-sharing activities like mentoring or teaching can also count towards fulfilling CPE requirements. By actively participating in CPE activities, CCSP professionals enhance their skills and knowledge, ensuring they remain effective in their roles and up-to-date with evolving technologies and threats in cloud security.

CPE Maintenance Fees:

CPE Maintenance Fees are annual fees paid by CCSP-certified professionals to maintain their certification status. These fees contribute to the administration and maintenance of the CCSP certification program by $(ISC)^2$. They support various activities, including processing CPE submissions, providing resources and support to certified professionals, upholding certification standards, and ensuring the ongoing relevance and credibility of the CCSP certification. It is essential for CCSP-certified professionals to timely pay these fees to retain their certification status and demonstrate their commitment to continuous professional development in cloud security.

Revocation of Certificate

Revocation of a certification, such as the Certified Cloud Security Professional (CCSP), is a serious action taken by the certifying authority, such as $(ISC)^2$, in response to various infractions or violations. This could include breaches of the code of ethics, failure to meet Continuing Education (CPE) requirements, misrepresentation of credentials, criminal convictions, or any other misconduct that undermines the integrity of the certification program. Before revoking a certification, the certifying body typically conducts thorough investigations and affords the individual an opportunity to respond to the allegations. Revocation signifies the loss of the right to use the certification credentials and requires the individual to cease representing themselves as certified. It is a consequential decision made after careful consideration, usually following established processes and procedures outlined by the certifying organization. Individuals facing revocation may have the opportunity to appeal or seek reinstatement through specified channels. Overall, revocation underscores the importance of upholding the standards and integrity of professional certifications in maintaining trust and credibility within the industry.

CCSP Exam Preparation Pointers

Preparing for the Certified Cloud Security Professional (CCSP) exam requires a comprehensive approach to ensure readiness and confidence on exam day. Here are some pointers to guide your CCSP exam preparation:

- **Understand the Exam Content:** Familiarize yourself with the domains and topics outlined in the CCSP exam content outline provided by (ISC)². This will give you a clear understanding of what to expect on the exam and which areas to focus your study efforts on.
- **Utilize Study Materials:** Make use of a variety of CCSP study materials, including textbooks, official (ISC)² publications, online courses, and practice exams. These resources will help reinforce your understanding of cloud security concepts and provide valuable insights into exam format and question types.
- **Take Practice Exams:** Completing CCSP practice exams is crucial for assessing your knowledge and identifying areas that require further study. Practice exams simulate the exam environment and help you gauge your readiness while familiarizing yourself with the types of questions you may encounter.
- **Create a Study Schedule:** Develop a study schedule that allocates time for reviewing each domain covered in the CCSP exam content outline. Set realistic study goals and deadlines to keep yourself accountable and ensure thorough coverage of all exam topics.
- **Join Study Groups:** Consider joining CCSP study groups or online forums where you can engage with other exam candidates, share resources, and discuss challenging topics. Collaborating with peers

can provide additional insights and support throughout your exam preparation journey.

- **Stay Updated:** Keep abreast of developments in cloud security by staying updated with industry trends, best practices, and emerging technologies. Attend relevant training sessions, workshops, and conferences to expand your knowledge and skills in this rapidly evolving field.
- **Practice Time Management:** During the exam, manage your time effectively by pacing yourself and allocating sufficient time to answer each question. Flag difficult questions for review and prioritize your efforts based on question weight and difficulty.
- **Stay Calm and Focused:** Maintain a calm and focused mindset on exam day. Take deep breaths, read each question carefully, and avoid becoming overwhelmed by difficult questions. Trust in your preparation and approach each question methodically.

By following these pointers and dedicating yourself to thorough exam preparation, you will be well-equipped to succeed on the CCSP exam and demonstrate your expertise in cloud security management.

Job Opportunities with CCSP Certifications

Obtaining a Certified Cloud Security Professional (CCSP) certification can open up various job opportunities in the field of cloud security. Here are some roles where CCSP certification is highly valued:

Cloud Architect

Designs and oversees the secure implementation of cloud solutions, ensuring they meet business needs and security best practices.

Cloud Engineer

Builds, configures, and maintains cloud infrastructure and applications, focusing on security and performance.

Cloud Consultant

Advises companies on cloud adoption strategies, security considerations, and migration processes.

Cloud Administrator

Manages day-to-day operations of cloud environments, including security configurations, user access, and resource allocation.

Cloud Security Analyst

Identifies, assesses, and mitigates security risks in cloud environments, ensuring compliance with regulations.

Cloud Specialist

Possesses in-depth knowledge of a specific cloud platform (AWS, Azure, GCP) and implements secure solutions within that platform.

Auditor of Cloud Computing Services

Performs security audits of cloud environments to ensure they meet control objectives and identify potential vulnerabilities.

Professional Cloud Developer

Develops secure and scalable cloud-based applications following secure coding practices.

These are just a few examples of the many job opportunities available to individuals with CISM certification. The demand for cybersecurity professionals continues to grow, and obtaining relevant certifications like CISM can significantly enhance your career prospects in this field.

Demand for CCSP Certification in 2024

The demand for CCSP certification in 2024 is expected to remain strong. Here is why:

- **Growing Cloud Security Market:** The cloud security market is booming, projected to reach $125 billion by 2032 [Infosec Institute].

This translates to a high demand for skilled professionals who can secure cloud environments.

- **Critical Skillset:** Earning a CCSP demonstrates expertise in securing cloud data, applications, and infrastructure, a critical skillset for businesses increasingly reliant on the cloud.

- **Competitive Advantage:** The CCSP certification sets you apart from other candidates and can lead to higher earning potential and career advancement opportunities.

Practice Questions

1.   Which of the following is not a standard cloud service model?

A) Software as a Service

B) Programming as a Service

C) Infrastructure as a Service

D) Platform as a Service

2.   All of these technologies have made cloud service viable except:

A) Virtualization

B) Widely available broadband

C) Cryptographic connectivity

D) Smart hubs

3.   Cloud vendors are held to contractual obligations with specified metrics by which one of the following:

A) SLAs

B) Regulations

C) Law

D) Discipline

4.   What drives security decisions in cloud computing?

A) Customer service responses

B) Surveys

C) Business requirements

D) Public opinion

5.   If a cloud customer cannot access the cloud provider, this affects what portion of the CIA triad?

A) Integrity

B) Authentication

C) Confidentiality

D) Availability

6.   Cloud Access Security Brokers (CASBs) might offer all the following services except:

A) Single Sign-On

B) BC/DR/COOP

C) IAM

D) Key escrow

7.   Encryption can be used in various aspects of cloud computing, including all of these except:

A) Storage

B) Remote access

C) Secure sessions

D) Magnetic swipe cards

8.   All of these are reasons an organization may want to consider cloud migration, except:

A) Reduced personnel costs

B) Elimination of risks

C) Reduced operational expenses

D) Increased efficiency

9.   The generally accepted definition of cloud computing includes all of the following characteristics except:

A) On-demand services

B) Negating the need for backups

C) Resource pooling

D) Measured or metered service

10.   All of the following can result in vendor lock-in except:

A) Unfavorable contract

B) Statutory compliance

C) Proprietary data formats

D) Insufficient bandwidth

11.   The risk that a cloud provider might go out of business and the cloud customer might not be able to recover data is known as:

A) Vendor closure

B) Vendor lock-out

C) Vendor lock-in

D) Vending route

12.   All of these are features of cloud computing except:

A) Broad network access

B) Reversed charging configuration

C) Rapid scaling

D) On-demand self-service

13.   When a cloud customer uploads PII to a cloud provider, who becomes ultimately responsible for the security of that PII?

A) Cloud provider

B) Regulators

C) Cloud customer

D) The individuals who are the subjects of the PII

14.   We use which of the following to determine an organization's critical paths, processes, and assets?

A) Business requirements

B) BIA

C) RMF

D) CIA triad

15.   The cloud deployment model that features organizational ownership of the hardware and infrastructure and usage only by members of that organization is known as:

A) Private

B) Public

C) Hybrid

D) Motive

16.   The cloud deployment model that features ownership by a cloud provider, with services offered to anyone who wants to subscribe, is known as:

A) Private

B) Public

C) Hybrid

D) Latent

17.   The cloud deployment model that features joint ownership of assets among an affinity the group is known as:

A) Private

B) Public

C) Hybrid

D) Community

18.   If a cloud customer requires a secure, isolated sandbox to conduct software development and testing, which cloud service model would probably be best?

A) IaaS

B) PaaS

C) SaaS

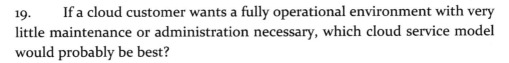

D) Hybrid

19.   If a cloud customer wants a fully operational environment with very little maintenance or administration necessary, which cloud service model would probably be best?

A) IaaS

B) PaaS

C) SaaS

D) Hybrid

20.   What cloud service model would probably be best if a cloud customer wants a bare-bones environment to replicate their enterprise for BC/DR purposes?

A) IaaS

B) PaaS

C) SaaS

D) Hybrid

21.   What are the key characteristics of cloud computing according to the NIST definition?

A) Limited access, manual services, static pooling, fixed service

B) Broad network access, on-demand services, resource pooling, measured service

C) Narrow network access, scheduled services, isolated pooling, unlimited service

D) Private network access, batch services, shared pooling, unlimited service

22.   Which cloud service model allows customers to install their software and operating systems on vendor-provided hardware?

A) Infrastructure as a Service (IaaS)

B) Platform as a Service (PaaS)

C) Software as a Service (SaaS)

D) Community Cloud

23.   What does "elasticity" refer to in cloud computing?

A) The simplicity of cloud service usage and administration

B) The ability to allocate resources as needed for immediate usage

C) The scalability of an organization's computing needs

D) The shared ownership of cloud resources among different entities

24.   Which cloud deployment model involves resources owned and operated by an affinity group for joint tasks and functions?

A) Public Cloud

B) Private Cloud

C) Community Cloud

D) Hybrid Cloud

25.   Who is responsible for administering, patching, and updating software in the Software as a Service (SaaS) model?

A) Cloud Customer

B) Cloud Access Security Broker (CASB)

C) Cloud Service Provider (CSP)

D) Regulators

26. What is the primary driver pushing organizations toward cloud migration?

A) Increased control over data security

B) Reduction in operational costs

C) Compliance with regulatory mandates

D) Enhanced data backup capabilities

27. Which method for gathering business requirements involves collecting financial records and marketing data?

A) Interviewing functional managers

B) Surveying customers

C) Collecting financial records

D) Collecting network traffic

28. In the context of cloud computing, what is the role of a Cloud Architect?

A) Providing independent identity and access management services

B) Developing software applications for cloud deployment

C) Managing cloud computing infrastructure and deployment

D) Ensuring compliance with regulatory frameworks

29.   Which cloud service model includes everything in Infrastructure as a Service (IaaS), in addition to operating systems?

A) Infrastructure as a Service (IaaS)

B) Platform as a Service (PaaS)

C) Software as a Service (SaaS)

D) Community Cloud

30.   What does the term "cloud bursting" refers to?

A) The sudden collapse of cloud computing infrastructure

B) The simultaneous deployment of multiple cloud services

C) Augmenting internal data center capabilities with managed services during times of increased demand

D) Transferring certain regulatory costs to a cloud provider

31.   Which of the following is NOT an essential characteristic of cloud computing according to the NIST definition?

A) Broad network access

B) On-demand services

C) Fixed resource pooling

D) Measured service

32.   What is the primary function of a Cloud Access Security Broker (CASB)?

A) Providing cloud computing infrastructure

B) Administering software applications in the cloud

C) Offering independent identity and access management services

D) Ensuring compliance with regulatory frameworks

33.	Which cloud deployment model is exclusively owned and operated by a specific organization?

A) Public Cloud

B) Private Cloud

C) Community Cloud

D) Hybrid Cloud

34.	What is the purpose of conducting a Business Impact Analysis (BIA)?

A) To evaluate the financial benefits of cloud migration

B) To assess the priorities of each asset and process within an organization

C) To determine the costs of compliance with regulatory mandates

D) To identify critical paths and single points of failure within an organization

35.	Which cloud service model involves the customer administering all logical resources, including software and operating systems?

A) Infrastructure as a Service (IaaS)

B) Platform as a Service (PaaS)

C) Software as a Service (SaaS)

D) Community Cloud

36.	What is the primary benefit of cloud migration?

VERSAtile Reads

A) Enhanced data backup capabilities

B) Increased control over data security

C) Reduction in personnel costs

D) Compliance with regulatory mandates

37. Which method for gathering business requirements involves interviewing senior management?

A) Interviewing functional managers

B) Surveying customers

C) Interviewing senior management

D) Collecting network traffic

38. Which cloud service model involves the customer only uploading and processing data on a complete production environment hosted by the provider?

A) Infrastructure as a Service (IaaS)

B) Platform as a Service (PaaS)

C) Software as a Service (SaaS)

D) Community Cloud

39. What is the term used to describe using a cloud-based service for data archival and disaster recovery purposes?

A) Cloud bursting

B) Cloud backup

C) Cloud architecting

VERSAtile Reads

D) Cloud migration

40.   Which of the following is NOT a method for gathering business requirements mentioned in the text?

A) Collecting financial records

B) Interviewing functional managers

C) Analyzing network traffic

D) Surveying customers

41.   What is the primary responsibility of regulators in the context of cloud computing?

A) Administering cloud service providers

B) Ensuring compliance with regulatory frameworks

C) Offering independent identity and access management services

D) Providing infrastructure and processing for cloud environments

42.   Which cloud deployment model combines elements of both public and private clouds?

A) Public Cloud

B) Private Cloud

C) Community Cloud

D) Hybrid Cloud

43.   What is the primary purpose of a Cloud Service Provider (CSP)?

A) Offering independent identity and access management services

B) Administering software applications in the cloud

C) Providing infrastructure and processing for cloud environments

D) Ensuring compliance with regulatory frameworks

44. Which cloud service model offers the highest level of control to the cloud customer?

A) Infrastructure as a Service (IaaS)

B) Platform as a Service (PaaS)

C) Software as a Service (SaaS)

D) Community Cloud

45. What is the main advantage of using a Cloud Access Security Broker (CASB)?

A) Cost savings in cloud service subscriptions

B) Enhanced control over data security

C) Simplified management of cloud resources

D) Independent identity and access management services

46. What does "simplicity" refer to in cloud computing?

A) The scalability of cloud resources

B) The flexibility of resource allocation

C) The ease of using and administering cloud services

D) The shared ownership of cloud resources

47.   Which cloud service model involves the cloud provider being responsible for administering software applications and hardware resources?

A) Infrastructure as a Service (IaaS)

B) Platform as a Service (PaaS)

C) Software as a Service (SaaS)

D) Community Cloud

48.   What is the primary function of a Business Impact Analysis (BIA)?

A) Assessing the financial benefits of cloud migration

B) Evaluating the priorities of each asset and process within an organization

C) Determining the costs of regulatory compliance

D) Identifying critical paths and single points of failure within an organization

49.   Which cloud characteristic allows customers to scale their computing and storage needs with little or no intervention from the provider?

A) Broad network access

B) On-demand services

C) Resource pooling

D) Measured service

50.   What is the main distinction between a cloud customer and a cloud user?

A) A cloud customer owns the cloud infrastructure, while a cloud user accesses it.

B) A cloud customer purchases services while a cloud user administers them.

C) A cloud customer provides cloud services while a cloud user consumes them.

D) A cloud customer leases cloud resources while a cloud user accesses them.

51.   Which cloud service model is most suitable for organizations looking to retain control over the security of their data?

A) Infrastructure as a Service (IaaS)

B) Platform as a Service (PaaS)

C) Software as a Service (SaaS)

D) Community Cloud

52.   What is the primary function of a Cloud Access Security Broker (CASB) in cloud computing?

A) Providing infrastructure and processing for cloud environments

B) Offering independent identity and access management services

C) Enhancing control over data security

D) Administering software applications in the cloud

53.   Which cloud deployment model is characterized by infrastructure owned and operated by independent organizations for exclusive use?

A) Public Cloud

B) Private Cloud

C) Community Cloud

D) Hybrid Cloud

54. What does "elasticity" refer to in cloud computing?

A) The flexibility of resource allocation

B) The ease of using and administering cloud services

C) The transparency of cloud service usage

D) The scalability of cloud resources

55. Which cloud service model involves the provider administering software applications and hardware resources?

A) Infrastructure as a Service (IaaS)

B) Platform as a Service (PaaS)

C) Software as a Service (SaaS)

D) Community Cloud

56. What is the primary purpose of a Cloud Service Provider (CSP)?

A) Ensuring compliance with regulatory frameworks

B) Administering software applications in the cloud

C) Offering independent identity and access management services

D) Providing infrastructure and processing for cloud environments

57. Which cloud characteristic allows customers to pay only for the resources they use?

A) Broad network access

B) On-demand services

C) Resource pooling

D) Measured service

58.   What is the primary advantage of using a hybrid cloud deployment model?

A) Enhanced control over data security

B) Cost savings in cloud service subscriptions

C) Flexibility to leverage both private and public cloud resources

D) Simplified management of cloud resources

59.   What is the primary objective of the chapter "Design Requirements"?

A) To introduce cloud computing concepts

B) To discuss architectural principles in cloud security

C) To explore data encryption strategies

D) To analyze risks associated with cloud infrastructure

60.   What is the first step in creating a sound security program?

A) Conducting a risk assessment

B) Performing a comprehensive inventory of assets

C) Implementing encryption strategies

D) Analyzing critical paths and processes

61.   What is the purpose of a Business Impact Analysis (BIA)?

A) To determine the value of assets

B) To identify critical aspects of the organization

C) To assess risks associated with cloud migration

D) To analyze data pathways within the organization

62.   Which of the following is an example of an intangible asset?

A) IT hardware

B) Retail Inventory

C) Intellectual property

D) Vehicles

63.   What is the significance of determining criticality in the context of Business Impact Analysis (BIA)?

A) It helps identify assets for encryption

B) It assists in risk mitigation strategies

C) It determines which assets require redundancy

D) It identifies aspects necessary for the organization's operation

64.   Which statement best describes the concept of Risk Appetite?

A) It is the level of risk that organizations find unacceptable

B) It is the likelihood of a risk being realized

C) It varies widely among organizations based on internal and external factors

D) It remains constant over time for all organizations

65.   What is the primary way for organizations to address risk?

A) Avoidance

B) Acceptance

C) Transference

D) Mitigation

66.   In cloud computing, what does IaaS stands for?

A) Infrastructure as a Service

B) Integration as a Service

C) Interface as a Service

D) Implementation as a Service

67.   What is a characteristic of the Platform as a Service (PaaS) cloud model?

A) The provider is responsible for managing the operating system

B) The customer has control over the hardware infrastructure

C) The customer manages all aspects of the environment, including the OS

D) The provider does not offer any security measures

68.   What is the recommended approach for securing devices in a cloud environment?

A) Implementing physical solid access controls

B) Installing monitoring equipment on the provider's infrastructure

C) Enforcing strict background checks for all personnel

D) Treating all cloud-related devices as if they are in the DMZ

69.   Which statement best describes the concept of homomorphic encryption?

A) It involves encrypting data during communication between cloud providers and users

B) It allows data to be processed in the cloud without decryption, preserving the confidentiality

C) It ensures physical security measures are implemented at the cloud provider's data center

D) It involves transferring the responsibility of data protection to the cloud provider

70.   What is the primary purpose of layered defenses in cloud security?

A) To enforce strict access control policies

B) To ensure the physical security of data centers

C) To implement multiple overlapping security measures

D) To transfer risk to third-party providers

71.   What is a recommended measure for securing BYOD assets accessing the cloud?

A) Disabling VPN solutions

B) Removing all security software

C) Implementing weak password policies

D) Utilizing data loss prevention (DLP) solutions

72.   Which cloud service model grants the customer the most responsibility and authority?

A) Infrastructure as a Service (IaaS)

B) Platform as a Service (PaaS)

C) Software as a Service (SaaS)

D) None of the above

73.   What is the primary purpose of hardening devices in a cloud environment?

A) To increase administrative privileges

B) To decrease network performance

C) To reduce the attack surface

D) To limit encryption capabilities

74.   How does the cloud customer's control change in the Platform as a Service (PaaS) model compared to the Infrastructure as a Service (IaaS) model?

A) The customer has more control over the operating system

B) The customer has less control over the hardware infrastructure

C) The customer has more control over the data storage

D) The customer has less control over the software applications

75.   What is the role of the cloud customer in the Software as a Service (SaaS) model?

A) To manage the hardware infrastructure

B) To install and maintain the operating system

C) To administer the software and data

D) To provide physical security for the data center

76.   How does the concept of risk appetite relate to organizations' risk acceptance?

A) It determines the level of risk that organizations find acceptable

B) It remains constant over time for all organizations

C) It is influenced by external factors only

D) It dictates the actions organizations take to mitigate risk

77.   What is the purpose of the Business Impact Analysis (BIA) process?

A) To identify single points of failure

B) To determine the value of assets

C) To analyze risks associated with cloud infrastructure

D) To assess critical paths and processes

78.   What is a crucial consideration for cloud customers in dealing with risks associated with physical access to data?

A) Implementing strict background checks for all personnel

B) Utilizing encryption for data in transit

C) Ensuring strong access controls for BYOD assets

D) Implementing measures to reduce the likelihood of breaches

79.   What is an example of a tangible asset?

A) Copyrights

B) Trademarks

C) Land

D) Patents

80.   What is the primary goal of the risk management process?

A) To eliminate all risks

B) To transfer all risks to third parties

C) To reduce risks to an acceptable level

D) To increase risks for potential gains

81.   In cloud computing, what does SaaS stand for?

A) Software as a Service

B) Security as a Service

C) Storage as a Service

D) Server as a Service

82.   What is a characteristic of the Software as a Service (SaaS) cloud model?

A) The customer manages all aspects of the environment, including the operating system

B) The provider is responsible for managing the hardware infrastructure

C) The customer has control over the software applications and data

D) The provider does not offer any service-level agreements

83.   What is the benefit of the Platform as a Service (PaaS) cloud model?

A) The customer has complete control over the underlying infrastructure

B) The provider manages the operating system and hardware, reducing customer responsibilities

C) The customer has direct access to physical servers in the data center

D) The provider does not offer any support for software development

84.   What is an example of a risk mitigation strategy?

A) Accepting all identified risks

B) Ignoring potential risks

C) Transferring risks to a third party

D) Amplifying risks for potential gains

85.   What is the purpose of encryption in cloud security?

A) To increase network performance

B) To decrease data availability

C) To protect data confidentiality and integrity

D) To limit access to cloud resources

86.   What is the role of encryption in securing data in transit?

A) To protect data while stored in cloud databases

B) To prevent unauthorized access to cloud resources

C) To secure data while it is being transmitted between network devices

D) To enforce access control policies for cloud users

87.   Which statement best describes the concept of risk tolerance?

A) It refers to the level of risk that organizations find unacceptable

B) It remains constant over time for all organizations

C) It is influenced by external factors only

D) It indicates the level of risk that organizations are willing to accept

88.   How does the concept of shared responsibility apply to cloud security?

A) The cloud provider is solely responsible for all security measures

B) The cloud customer is solely responsible for all security measures

C) Both the cloud provider and the customer share responsibility for security

D) Security responsibility is transferred to a third-party provider

89.   What is the primary purpose of conducting a Business Impact Analysis (BIA) in the context of security?

A) To identify critical assets within the organization

B) To determine the financial value of each asset

C) To evaluate the effectiveness of security controls

D) To assess the level of risk appetite

90.   Which of the following is NOT an example of a critical aspect within an organization?

A) Tangible assets

B) Intangible assets

C) Non-essential personnel

D) Key business processes

91.   What is a Single Point of Failure (SPOF) in risk management?

A) A process that is essential for the organization's operations

B) A vulnerability that increases the likelihood of a security breach

C) A weakness that could fail an entire system

D) A control measure that mitigates the impact of a security incident

92.   How can organizations address their infrastructure's Single Points of Failure (SPOFs)?

A) By increasing the likelihood of failures to spread risks

B) By reducing redundancy to streamline operations

C) By implementing alternative processes and redundancies

D) By ignoring potential weaknesses to focus on core activities

93.   What best defines the risk appetite?

A) It refers to the organization's willingness to accept high levels of risk

B) It determines the level of risk that is unacceptable to the organization

C) It represents the level of risk that the organization finds tolerable

D) It indicates the organization's ability to eliminate all risks

94.   Which of the following risk management strategies involves transferring risk to a third party?

A) Avoidance

B) Acceptance

C) Transference

D) Mitigation

95.   What is homomorphic encryption, and how does it relate to cloud security?

A) It is a method of encrypting data while in transit between cloud providers and users

B) It refers to the encryption of data stored within the cloud to protect confidentiality

C) It allows computations to be performed on encrypted data without decrypting it

D) It involves encrypting cloud infrastructure to prevent unauthorized access

96.   What is the purpose of hardening devices in the context of cloud security?

A) To make devices more susceptible to security breaches

B) To reduce the efficiency of security controls

C) To increase the complexity of managing cloud resources

D) To enhance the security of cloud infrastructure

97.   What is the significance of layered defenses in cloud security?

A) It focuses solely on physical security measures

B) It reduces the need for administrative controls

C) It provides multiple overlapping security measures

D) It eliminates the need for encryption technologies

98.   Gathering business requirements can aid the organization in determining all of this information about organizational assets, except:

A) Full inventory

B) Usefulness

C) Value

D) Criticality

99.   The BIA can be used to provide information about all the following, except:

A) Risk analysis

B) Secure acquisition

C) BC/DR planning

D) Selection of security controls

100.   In which cloud service model is the customer required to maintain the OS?

A) CaaS

B) SaaS

C) PaaS

D) IaaS

101.   In which cloud service model is the customer required to maintain and update only the applications?

A) CaaS

B) SaaS

C) PaaS

D) IaaS

102.   In which cloud service model is the customer only responsible for the data?

A) CaaS

B) SaaS

C) PaaS

D) IaaS

103.   The cloud customer and provider negotiate their respective responsibilities and rights regarding the capabilities and data of the cloud service. Where is the eventual agreement codified?

A) RMF

B) Contract

C) MOU

D) BIA

104.   In attempting to provide a layered defense, the security practitioner should convince senior management to include security controls of which type?

A) Technological

B) Physical

C) Administrative

D) All of the above

105.　Which of the following is considered an administrative control?

A) Access control process

B) Keystroke logging

C) Door locks

D) Biometric authentication

106.　Which of the following is considered a technological control?

A) Firewall software

B) Fireproof safe

C) Fire extinguisher

D) Firing personnel

107.　Which of the following is considered a physical control?

A) Carpets

B) Ceilings

C) Doors

D) Fences

108.　In a cloud environment, encryption should be used for all the following except:

A) Long-term storage of data

B) Near-term storage of virtualized images

C) Secure sessions/VPN

D) Profile formatting

109.   The process of hardening a device should include all the following:

A) Improve default accounts

B) Close unused ports

C) Delete unnecessary services

D) Strictly control administrator access

E) All of the above

110.   The process of hardening a device should include which of the following?

A) Encrypting the OS

B) Updating and patching the system

C) Using video cameras

D) Performing thorough personnel background checks

111.   What is an experimental technology that is intended to create the possibility of processing encrypted data without having to decrypt it first?

A) Homomorphic

B) Polyinstantiation

C) Quantum-state

D) Gastronomic

112.   Risk appetite for an organization is determined by which of the following?

A) Appetite evaluation

B) Senior management

C) Legislative mandates

D) Contractual agreement

113.   What is the risk left over after controls and countermeasures are implemented?

A) Null

B) High

C) Residual

D) Pertinent

114.   All the following are ways of addressing risk, except:

A) Acceptance

B) Reversal

C) Mitigation

D) Transfer

115.   To protect data on user devices in a BYOD environment, the organization should consider requiring all the following, except:

A) DLP agents

B) Local encryption

C) Multi-factor authentication

D) Two-person integrity

116.   Devices in the cloud data center should be secure against attack. All the following are means of hardening devices, except:

A) Using a firm password policy

B) Removing default passwords

C) Strictly limiting physical access

D) Removing all admin accounts

117.   Which of the following best describes risk?

A) Preventable

B) Everlasting

C) The likelihood that a threat will exploit a vulnerability

D) Transient

118.   Which model is used by the military for data classification based on sensitivity?

A) Functional Unit

B) Jurisdiction

C) Criticality

D) Sensitivity

119.   What aspect of data classification is determined by the geophysical location of data?

A) Sensitivity

B) Jurisdiction

C) Criticality

D) Business Function

120. What information might be included in data labels?

A) Date of destruction only

B) Access limitations only

C) Source and applicable regulation

D) Dissemination instructions only

121. What is the term for collecting electronic evidence for an investigation or lawsuit?

A) Data Inventory

B) Data Classification

C) Data Discovery

D) Data Labeling

122. How do labels aid in data discovery efforts?

A) By hindering the identification of data

B) By providing accurate and sufficient information

C) By complicating the process of data identification

D) By slowing down the data discovery process

123. Which method of data discovery relies heavily on the labels created by data owners?

A) Label-Based Discovery

B) Jurisdiction-Based Discovery

C) Sensitivity-Based Discovery

D) Functional Unit-Based Discovery

124.   What is the main reason for creating data labels?

A) To disclose the data they describe

B) To indicate individual names or identities

C) To hinder security efforts

D) To communicate pertinent concepts

125.   What is the primary responsibility of data owners during the Create phase of the data lifecycle?

A) Manipulating data

B) Assigning data custodians

C) Understanding data usage

D) Identifying themselves

126.   Which phase of the data lifecycle involves identifying data custodians?

A) Create

B) Store

C) Archive

D) Destroy

127.   What role does the cloud provider typically play in data ownership?

A) Data custodian

B) Data owner

C) Data processor

D) Data controller

128.   How can labels aid in data security efforts?

A) By complicating data handling

B) By obscuring data sensitivity

C) By indicating how data should be handled

D) By reducing data accessibility

129.   What is the primary purpose of data categorization?

A) To enforce ad hoc categorization

B) To have no categorization at all

C) To understand how data will be used

D) To arbitrarily assign categories

130.   In what phase of the data lifecycle does data classification take place?

A) Store

B) Archive

C) Create

D) Destroy

131.   What is the primary trait used for data classification?

A) Sensitivity

B) Jurisdiction

C) Criticality

D) Business Function

132.   Which information might NOT be included in data labels?

A) Handling directions

B) Date of scheduled destruction/disposal

C) Access limitations

D) Data encryption method

133.   How can labels aid in data security efforts?

A) By complicating data handling

B) By obscuring data sensitivity

C) By indicating how data should be handled

D) By reducing data accessibility

134.   What is the primary purpose of data discovery?

A) To assign data ownership

B) To determine data sensitivity

C) To create data labels

D) To identify and inventory data

135.   154. Which method of data discovery relies on the physical location of data sources or storage points?

A) Jurisdiction-Based Discovery

B) Label-Based Discovery

C) Sensitivity-Based Discovery

D) Functional Unit-Based Discovery

136.   155. What is the primary purpose of data labeling?

A) To disclose individual identities

B) To hinder data discovery efforts

C) To communicate pertinent concepts

D) To obscure data characteristics

137.   156. What is the main objective of data classification according to the chapter?

A) To create data inventories

B) To assign responsibilities to data owners

C) To understand the data lifecycle

D) To properly allocate security resources

138.   157. Who is typically considered the data owner in a cloud computing context?

A) Cloud provider

B) Data custodian

C) Department head or business unit manager

D) Database administrator

139.   158. What is the responsibility of a data custodian?

A) Assigning data categories

B) Creating data inventories

C) Manipulating, storing, or moving data

D) Determining data lifecycle phases

140.   159. Which phase of the data lifecycle is primarily concerned with identifying the data owner?

A) Archive

B) Store

C) Create

D) Destroy

141.   160. What is the purpose of data categorization?

A) To determine data ownership

B) To create data labels

C) To understand how data will be used

D) To assign data custodians

142.   161. What is the primary purpose of data categorization?

A) To enforce ad hoc categorization

B) To have no categorization at all

C) To understand how data will be used

D) To arbitrarily assign categories

143.   162. In what phase of the data lifecycle does data classification take place?

A) Store

B) Archive

C) Create

D) Destroy

144.   163. What is the primary trait used for data classification?

A) Sensitivity

B) Jurisdiction

C) Criticality

D) Business Function

145.   Which information might NOT be included in data labels?
A) Handling directions

B) Date of scheduled destruction/disposal

C) Access limitations

D) Data encryption method

146.   How can labels aid in data security efforts?
A) By complicating data handling

B) By obscuring data sensitivity

C) By indicating how data should be handled

D) By reducing data accessibility

147. What is the primary purpose of data discovery?
A) To assign data ownership

B) To determine data sensitivity

C) To create data labels

D) To identify and inventory data

148. Which method of data discovery relies on the physical location of data sources or storage points?
A) Jurisdiction-Based Discovery

B) Label-Based Discovery

C) Sensitivity-Based Discovery

D) Functional Unit-Based Discovery

149. What is the primary purpose of data labeling?
A) To disclose individual identities

B) To hinder data discovery efforts

C) To communicate pertinent concepts

D) To obscure data characteristics

150. What is the main objective of data classification according to the chapter?
A) To create data inventories

B) To assign responsibilities to data owners

C) To understand the data lifecycle

D) To properly allocate security resources

151.   Who is typically considered the data owner in a cloud computing context?

A) Cloud provider

B) Data custodian

C) Department head or business unit manager

D) Database administrator

152.   What is the responsibility of a data custodian?
A) Assigning data categories

B) Creating data inventories

C) Manipulating, storing, or moving data

D) Determining data lifecycle phases

153.   What is the primary purpose of a cloud access security broker (CASB) in cloud computing?
A) To manage cloud provider relationships
B) To provide encryption services for cloud data
C) To enforce security policies across cloud services
D) To optimize cloud infrastructure performance

154.   Which of the following authentication mechanisms provides the highest level of security for accessing cloud services?
A) Username and password
B) Biometric authentication
C) Single sign-on (SSO)
D) Security tokens

155.   In the context of cloud computing, what does the principle of least privilege entail?

A) Granting users access only to the data and resources required to perform their job functions

B) Allowing users unrestricted access to all cloud services and resources

C) Assigning administrative privileges to all users by default

D) Revoking access to cloud services and resources after a certain period of time

156.   Which phase of the data lifecycle is primarily concerned with identifying the data owner?

A) Archive

B) Store

C) Create

D) Destroy

157.   What is the purpose of data categorization?

A) To determine data ownership

B) To create data labels

C) To understand how data will be used

D) To assign data custodians

158.   In what phase of the data lifecycle does data classification take place?

A) Store

B) Archive

C) Create

D) Destroy

159.   What is the primary trait used for data classification?

A) Sensitivity

B) Jurisdiction

C) Criticality

D) Business Function

160.   Which information might NOT be included in data labels?

A) Handling directions

B) Date of scheduled destruction/disposal

C) Access limitations

D) Data encryption method

161.   How can labels aid in data security efforts?

A) By complicating data handling

B) By obscuring data sensitivity

C) By indicating how data should be handled

D) By reducing data accessibility

162.   Who is typically considered the data owner in a cloud computing context?

A) Cloud provider

B) Data custodian

C) Department head or business unit manager

D) Database administrator

163.   What is the responsibility of a data custodian?

A) Assigning data categories

B) Creating data inventories

C) Manipulating, storing, or moving data

D) Determining data lifecycle phases

164.   All of these are methods of data discovery, except:

A) Content-based

B) User-based

C) Label-based

D) Metadata-based

165.   Data labels could include all the following: except:

A) Date data was created

B) Data owner

C) Data value

D) Data of scheduled destruction

166.   Data labels could include all the following, except:

A) Source

B) Delivery vendor

C) Handling restrictions

D) Jurisdiction

167.   Data labels could include all the following, except:

A) Confidentiality level

B) Distribution limitations

C) Access restrictions

D) Multi-factor authentication

168.   All the following are data analytics modes, except:

A) Real-time analytics

B) Datamining

C) Agile business intelligence

D) Refractory iterations

169.   In the cloud motif, the data owner is usually:

A) In another jurisdiction

B) The cloud customer

C) The cloud provider

D) The cloud access security broker

170.   In the cloud motif, the data processor is usually:

A) The party that assigns access rights

B) The cloud customer

C) The cloud provider

D) The cloud access security broker

171.   Every security program and process should have which of the following?

A) Foundational policy

B) Severe penalties

C) Multi-factor authentication

D) Homomorphic encryption

172.   All policies within the organization should include a section that includes all of the following, except:

A) Policy maintenance

B) Policy review

C) Policy Enforcement

D) Policy adjudication

173.   Which of the following is the most pragmatic option for data disposal in the cloud?

A) Melting

B) Cryptoshredding

C) Cold fusion

D) Overwriting

174.   What is the intellectual property protection for the tangible expression of a creative idea?

A) Copyright

B) Patent

C) Trademark

D) Trade secret

175. What is the intellectual property protection for a practical manufacturing innovation?

A) Copyright

B) Patent

C) Trademark

D) Trade secret

176. What is the intellectual property protection for a valuable set of sales leads?

A) Copyright

B) Patent

C) Trademark

D) Trade secret

177. What is the intellectual property protection for a confidential recipe for muffins?

A) Copyright

B) Patent

C) Trademark

D) Trade secret

178.   What is the intellectual property protection for the logo of a new video game?

A) Copyright

B) Patent

C) Trademark

D) Trade secret

179.   What is the aspect of the DMCA that has often been abused and places the burden of proof on the accused?

A) Online service provider exemption

B) Decryption program prohibition

C) Takedown notice

D) Puppet plasticity

180.   What is the federal agency that accepts applications for new patents?

A) USDA

B) USPTO

C) OSHA

D) SEC

181.   DRM tools use a variety of methods for the enforcement of intellectual property rights. These include all the following except:

A) Support-based licensing

B) Local agent enforcement

C) Dip switch validity

D) Media-present checks

182.   All of the following regions have at least one country with an overarching federal privacy law protecting the personal data of its citizens, except:

A) Asia

B) Europe

C) South America

D) The United States

183.   DRM solutions should generally include all the following functions except:

A) Persistency

B) Automatic self-destruct

C) Automatic expiration

D) Dynamic policy control

184.   What security aspects must be carried over from legacy environments when migrating data to the cloud?

A) Availability and reliability

B) Authentication and authorization

C) Compliance and regulatory constraints

D) Encryption and decryption

185.   What does the data life cycle in the cloud have in common with the legacy environment?

VERSAtile Reads

A) Similarity in data storage techniques

B) Uniformity in data manipulation procedures

C) Consistency in data security requirements

D) Parallelism in data usage patterns

186.   What is the primary concern during the Create phase of the data life cycle in the cloud?

A) Data encryption

B) Data storage optimization

C) Data categorization and labeling

D) Data access control

187.   How should data created remotely by users be protected in the cloud environment?

A) By implementing multi-factor authentication

B) By using secure encryption methods

C) By restricting data access based on user roles

D) By employing robust intrusion detection systems

188.   What is emphasized as a critical consideration during the Store phase of the cloud data life cycle?

A) Data duplication

B) Data migration

C) Data encryption

D) Data compression

189.   What is a crucial requirement for securing data during the Use phase in the cloud environment?

A) Ensuring physical access control

B) Establishing data redundancy

C) Implementing a robust authentication mechanisms

D) Enforcing strict data retention policies

190.   What security measure is particularly relevant during the Share phase of the cloud data life cycle?

A) Encryption of shared files and communications

B) Implementation of data compression techniques

C) Deployment of intrusion prevention systems

D) Enforcement of data retention policies

191.   What is the purpose of export restrictions mentioned in the Share phase of the cloud data life cycle?

A) To regulate data migration between cloud providers

B) To prevent unauthorized access to sensitive data

C) To control the geographic distribution of data

D) To facilitate data sharing among authorized users

192.   Which scenario illustrates a potential risk of storing cloud backups in the same cloud environment as production data?

A) Increased risk of data duplication

B) Greater susceptibility to insider threats

C) Enhanced data accessibility for authorized users

D) Reduced likelihood of data loss during disaster recovery

193.   What is the recommended method for securely erasing data in the Destroy phase of the cloud data life cycle?

A) Physical destruction of storage media

B) Overwriting data with random patterns

C) Encrypting data using strong cryptographic algorithms

D) Deleting data using standard file deletion commands

194.   What distinguishes file storage from block storage in cloud storage architectures?

A) File storage offers higher performance than block storage.

B) Block storage provides a hierarchical structure for data organization.

C) File storage allows direct access to individual data blocks.

D) Block storage allows more flexibility but requires additional administration.

195.   Which cloud service model is volume storage, such as file and block storage, often associated with?

A) Software as a Service (SaaS)

B) Platform as a Service (PaaS)

C) Infrastructure as a Service (IaaS)

D) Function as a Service (FaaS)

196.   What data protection technique is commonly implemented in volume storage architectures to ensure resilience?

A) Data masking

B) Data encryption

C) Data deduplication

D) Data erasure coding

197.   What is the potential consequence of mismanaged cryptographic keys in cloud data archiving?

A) Reduced data redundancy

B) Increased data accessibility

C) Compromised data confidentiality

D) Enhanced data availability

198.   Why is it important to consider the format of data storage media in long-term archiving in the cloud?

A) To minimize data duplication

B) To optimize data compression

C) To ensure compatibility with legacy hardware

D) To prevent data degradation and obsolescence

199.   What personnel-related security measures should be considered when storing data with a third-party provider?

A) Background checks for provider staff

B) Employee training on data encryption

C) Access control based on job roles

D) Implementation of biometric authentication

200.   How can egress monitoring benefit data security during the Share phase of the cloud data life cycle?

A) By preventing unauthorized data access

B) By detecting and mitigating insider threats

C) By monitoring data traffic leaving the cloud environment

D) By enforcing data retention policies

201.   What is the primary function of export controls in cloud data sharing?

A) To enforce data access policies

B) To regulate data transmission across networks

C) To ensure compliance with international regulations

D) To prevent data loss during transmission

202.   What lesson can be learned from the case of the software repository company mentioned in the text?

A) The importance of implementing a robust encryption mechanisms

B) The necessity of segregating production and backup data in the cloud

C) The effectiveness of relying on third-party cloud providers for data security

D) The significance of regular data backups for disaster recovery

203.   What fundamental concept of data security is emphasized throughout the chapter about cloud data management?

A) Data availability

B) Data integrity

C) Data sovereignty

D) Data redundancy

204.   What role does encryption play in securing data during the Create phase of the cloud data life cycle?

A) It prevents unauthorized access to stored data.

B) It ensures the availability of data during transmission.

C) It protects data from being modified or tampered with.

D) It facilitates efficient data storage and retrieval.

205.   Which technology is recommended for securing data transmission during the Create phase of the cloud data life cycle?

A) IPSec VPN

B) SSL/TLS encryption

C) SSH tunneling

D) WPA2 encryption

206.   What is a primary consideration for ensuring secure remote access during the Use phase of the cloud data life cycle?

A) Implementing network segmentation

B) Enforcing strong password policies

C) Utilizing multi-factor authentication

D) Conducting regular vulnerability scans

207. What is the significance of data owners restricting permissions during the Use phase of the cloud data life cycle?

A) It prevents unauthorized data access.

B) It ensures compliance with data retention policies.

C) It facilitates efficient data sharing among users.

D) It minimizes the risk of data corruption.

208. Which international regulation is mentioned in the text as consideration for export restrictions during data sharing in the cloud?

A) GDPR (General Data Protection Regulation)

B) HIPAA (Health Insurance Portability and Accountability Act)

C) ITAR (International Traffic in Arms Regulations)

D) CCPA (California Consumer Privacy Act)

209. What does egress monitoring aim to achieve in the context of cloud data sharing?

A) Preventing data breaches

B) Monitoring data access patterns

C) Detecting unauthorized data exfiltration

D) Ensuring compliance with data retention policies

210.   What is a critical consideration for selecting a storage location during the Archive phase of the cloud data life cycle?

A) Network latency

B) Data deduplication

C) Disaster recovery capabilities

D) Physical and environmental security

211.   Why is critical management considered crucial during long-term data archiving in the cloud?

A) To ensure data availability

B) To maintain data redundancy

C) To protect data integrity

D) To safeguard data confidentiality

212.   What scenario exemplifies the importance of considering future data format compatibility during data archiving in the cloud?

A) Storing data in a proprietary format to prevent unauthorized access

B) Converting data into obsolete formats to reduce storage costs

C) Migrating data to cloud storage platforms with limited format support

D) Retaining data in formats accessible by legacy hardware and software

213.   What lesson can be derived from the case of the software repository company regarding cloud data backup strategies?

A) The necessity of encrypting data backups to prevent unauthorized access

B) The importance of storing cloud backups separately from production data

C) The effectiveness of relying solely on cloud-based disaster recovery solutions

D) The significance of maintaining multiple copies of backups in diverse locations

214.   What is the primary objective of cryptographic erasure (crypto shredding) during data destruction in the cloud?

A) To irreversibly delete data from storage media

B) To compress data for efficient storage utilization

C) To encrypt data to prevent unauthorized access

D) To mask data to preserve its confidentiality

215.   What distinguishes file storage from block storage regarding data organization in the cloud?

A) File storage offers a hierarchical structure, while block storage is unstructured.

B) Block storage provides advanced indexing capabilities compared to file storage.

C) File storage allows direct manipulation of individual data blocks.

D) Block storage enables seamless integration with legacy file systems.

216.   How does erasure coding contribute to data resilience in cloud storage architectures?

A) By reducing data redundancy

B) By enhancing data availability

C) By improving data compression efficiency

D) By minimizing data replication overhead

217. What risk is associated with the use of highly portable storage media in cloud volume storage architectures?

A) Data fragmentation

B) Data corruption

C) Data loss or theft

D) Data duplication

218. What personnel-related security measures should organizations consider when outsourcing data storage to third-party cloud providers?

A) Implementing role-based access controls

B) Conducting periodic security training for employees

C) Performing background checks on provider staff

D) Enforcing strict password policies

219. How does implementing data encryption in cloud storage contribute to regulatory compliance?

A) By ensuring data availability

B) By protecting data integrity

C) By safeguarding data confidentiality

D) By reducing data retention periods

220. What lesson can be learned from the case of the software repository company regarding cloud data backup strategies?

A) The necessity of encrypting data backups to prevent unauthorized access

B) The importance of storing cloud backups separately from production data

C) The effectiveness of relying solely on cloud-based disaster recovery solutions

D) The significance of maintaining multiple copies of backups in diverse locations

221. What distinguishes object storage from traditional file or block storage?

A) Objects include metadata and a unique identifier

B) Objects are stored in a sequential manner

C) Objects are accessed through APIs only

D) Objects are limited to a fixed size

222. Which cloud service model is most commonly associated with object storage architectures?

A) PaaS

B) SaaS

C) IaaS

D) FaaS

223. What is the primary purpose of homomorphic encryption in cloud computing?

A) To decrypt data for storage efficiency

B) To encrypt data in transit

C) To process encrypted data without decryption

D) To secure data access control

224.   Which technique is NOT used for obscuring data in the cloud?

A) Randomization

B) Hashing

C) Shuffling

D) Compression

225.   What is the primary purpose of a Security Information and Event Management (SIEM) system?

A) To manage cloud infrastructure

B) To enforce data access policies

C) To centralize the collection and analysis of log data

D) To encrypt data at rest

226.   What aspect of data storage is emphasized in object storage architectures?

A) Sequential access

B) Metadata and unique identifiers

C) Block-level encryption

D) File hierarchy structure

227.   In which cloud service model are databases most commonly implemented?

A) IaaS

B) PaaS

C) SaaS

D) DaaS

228.   What is the primary advantage of using a Content Delivery Network (CDN)?

A) Reduced storage costs

B) Improved data security

C) Faster data delivery to users

D) Increased data redundancy

229.   Which encryption method is used to protect data while it is being transmitted?

A) Homomorphic encryption

B) Key management

C) At-rest encryption

D) Encryption in transit

230.   What is a key consideration for key management in cloud computing?

A) Maximizing data availability

B) Storing encryption keys alongside the data

C) Maintaining low processing overhead

D) Securing encryption keys at the same level as the protected data

231.   What is the primary goal of Security Information and Event Management (SIEM) implementation?

A) Centralizing data storage

B) Automating data encryption

C) Enhancing log analysis capabilities

D) Implementing network firewalls

232.   What is the purpose of egress monitoring in cloud security?

A) To prevent unauthorized access to data

B) To monitor incoming network traffic

C) To examine data as it leaves the production environment

D) To enforce data access policies

233.   Which technology allows for processing encrypted data without decryption first?

A) Key management

B) Homomorphic encryption

C) Content Delivery Network (CDN)

D) Tokenization.

234.   What is a critical challenge in implementing Data Loss Prevention (DLP) solutions in cloud environments?

A) Lack of encryption standards

B) High processing overhead

C) Limited network bandwidth

D) Insufficient access permissions

235.   Which cloud service model is best suited for implementing databases?

A) Infrastructure as a Service (IaaS)

B) Platform as a Service (PaaS)

C) Software as a Service (SaaS)

D) Database as a Service (DaaS)

236.   What does a Content Delivery Network (CDN) primarily aim to improve?

A) Data integrity

B) Data Privacy

C) Data availability

D) Data latency

237.   What role does critical management play in cloud security?

A) Protecting data during transmission

B) Storing encryption keys alongside data

C) Securing encryption keys at the same level as protected data

D) Encrypting data at rest

238.   How does homomorphic encryption differ from traditional encryption methods?

A) It encrypts data at rest and in transit simultaneously

83

B) It allows the processing of encrypted data without decryption

C) It requires the use of physical hardware security modules

D) It uses symmetric encryption algorithms exclusively

239.   What is the primary advantage of using a Security Information and Event Management (SIEM) system?

A) Increased data storage capacity

B) Enhanced log analysis capabilities

C) Automated data encryption

D) Real-time network monitoring

240.   Which technique is NOT used for obscuring sensitive data in cloud environments?

A) Shuffling

B) Tokenization

C) Hashing

D) Compression

241.   Which cloud storage architecture is primarily associated with storing data as objects?

A) File storage

B) Block storage

C) Object storage

D) Database storage

242. In which cloud service model are databases most commonly configured to work?

A) Infrastructure as a Service (IaaS)

B) Platform as a Service (PaaS)

C) Software as a Service (SaaS)

D) Database as a Service (DaaS)

243. What is the primary purpose of a Content Delivery Network (CDN)?

A) Data encryption

B) Data replication

C) Data compression

D) Data latency reduction

244. What is the primary function of key management in cloud security?

A) Ensuring data availability

B) Securing encryption keys at the same level as protected data

C) Encrypting data during transmission

D) Storing encryption keys alongside data

245. What distinguishes homomorphic encryption from traditional encryption methods?

A) It encrypts data at rest and in transit simultaneously

B) It allows processing of encrypted data without decryption

C) It requires the use of physical hardware security modules

D) It uses symmetric encryption algorithms exclusively

246.   What is the primary advantage of using a Security Information and Event Management (SIEM) system?

A) Increased data storage capacity

B) Enhanced log analysis capabilities

C) Automated data encryption

D) Real-time network monitoring

247.   DLP can be combined with what other security technology to enhance data controls?

A) DRM

B) SIEM

C) Kerberos

D) Hypervisors

248.   What are the U.S. State Department controls on technology exports known as?

A) ITAR

B) EAR

C) EAL

D) DRM

249.   What are the U.S. Commerce Department controls on technology exports known as?

A) ITAR

B) EAR

C) EAL

D) DRM

250. Cryptographic keys for encrypted data stored in the cloud should be:

A) At least 128 bits long

B) Not stored with the cloud provider

C) Split into groups

D) Generated with redundancy

251. Best practices for key management include all of the following, except:

A) Have key recovery processes

B) Maintain critical security

C) Pass-keys out of the band

D) Ensure Multi-factor authentication

252. Cryptographic keys should be secured:

A) To a level at least as high as the data they can decrypt

B) In vaults

C) By armed guards

D) With two-person integrity

253. When crafting plans and policies for data archiving, we should consider all of the following, except:

A) Archive location

B) The backup process

C) The format of the data

D) Immediacy of the technology

254.   What is the correct order of the phases of the data life cycle?

A) Create, Store, Use, Archive, Share, Destroy

B) Create, Store, Use, Share, Archive, Destroy

C) Create, Use, Store, Share, Archive, Destroy

D) Create, Archive, Store, Share, Use, Destroy

255.   What are third-party providers of IAM functions for the cloud environment?

A) DLPs

B) CASBs

C) SIEMs

D) AESs

256.   What is a cloud storage architecture that manages the data in a hierarchy of files?

A) Object-based storage

B) File-based storage

C) Database

D) CDN

257.   What is a cloud storage architecture that manages the data in caches of copied content close to locations of high demand?

A) Object-based storage

B) File-based storage

C) Database

D) CDN

258.   Which domain of cloud computing does the chapter primarily focus on?

A) Cloud Platform and Infrastructure Security

B) Legal and Compliance

C) Architectural Concepts and Design Requirements

D) Data Management and Governance

259.   What is the ultimate legal liability for unauthorized data disclosures in cloud computing?

A) Shared equally between the cloud provider and customer

B) Solely with the cloud provider

C) Solely with the cloud customer as the data owner

D) Transferred to the regulatory authority

260.   What is one potential consequence for the cloud customer in case of an unauthorized data disclosure event?

A) Decrease in the cloud provider's share price

B) Increased market share for the cloud customer

C) Adverse effects on the cloud customer's clientele faith

D) Reduction in insurance premiums for the cloud customer

261.   Which cloud deployment model provides an organization with the highest level of autonomy and authority?

A) Public Cloud

B) Private Cloud

C) Community Cloud

D) Hybrid Cloud

262.   What is one risk associated with vendor lock-in in cloud computing?

A) Increased data portability

B) Decreased dependency on the cloud provider

C) Potential inability to migrate data to another provider

D) Enhanced flexibility in contract negotiations

263.   In cloud computing, what is the primary factor determining the division of responsibilities and risks between the cloud provider and the customer?

A) The size of the organization

B) The geographical location of the data center

C) The terms outlined in the service contract

D) The level of encryption used for data storage

264.   Which aspect of cloud computing is particularly emphasized when discussing risks associated with public cloud deployment?

A) Personnel threats

B) Vendor lock-in

C) Natural disasters

D) Regulatory non-compliance

265.   What is one advantage of a community cloud deployment model?

A) Centralized administration for performance and monitoring

B) Complete control over infrastructure and security

C) Shared costs among members of the community

D) Resilience to natural disasters

266.   Which cloud service model provides the highest level of control and autonomy for the cloud customer?

A) Infrastructure as a Service (IaaS)

B) Platform as a Service (PaaS)

C) Software as a Service (SaaS)

D) Hybrid Cloud

267.   What is one potential risk associated with regulatory noncompliance in cloud computing?

A) Loss of data due to natural disasters

B) Legal repercussions and fines

C) Decreased market share for the cloud provider

D) Increased transparency in data handling practices

268. How can an organization enhance the portability of its data in cloud computing?

A) By increasing vendor lock-in

B) By relying solely on proprietary data formats

C) By considering migration portability during planning

D) By limiting data encryption

269. Which deployment model is characterized by the organization controlling the entire infrastructure, including hardware, software, and security controls?

A) Public Cloud

B) Private Cloud

C) Community Cloud

D) Hybrid Cloud

270. What is the primary concern for organizations regarding vendor lock-in in cloud computing?

A) Increased data security

B) Decreased dependency on the cloud provider

C) Difficulty in migrating data to another provider

D) Enhanced flexibility in contract negotiations

271. What role does the service contract play in determining the division of responsibilities and risks between the cloud provider and the customer?

A) It does not influence on the division of responsibilities

B) It determines the geographical location of the data center

C) It primarily dictates the division of responsibilities and risks

D) It determines the level of encryption used for data storage

272.   Which cloud deployment model offers the most benefits regarding resilience to the loss of infrastructure nodes?

A) Public Cloud

B) Private Cloud

C) Community Cloud

D) Hybrid Cloud

273.   What is a potential consequence of regulatory noncompliance in cloud computing?

A) Increased data security measures

B) Legal repercussions and fines

C) Improved market share for the cloud provider

D) Enhanced customer trust and loyalty

274.   What is the primary benefit of a public cloud deployment model?

A) Complete control over infrastructure and security

B) Shared costs among members of the community

C) Reduced dependency on the cloud provider

D) Scalability and flexibility in resource allocation

275.   Which cloud service model involves the provider managing and maintaining the underlying infrastructure?

A) Infrastructure as a Service (IaaS)

B) Platform as a Service (PaaS)

C) Software as a Service (SaaS)

D) Hybrid Cloud

276.   What is one risk associated with natural disasters in cloud computing?

A) Decreased transparency in data handling practices

B) Loss of data due to physical damage to infrastructure

C) Increased control over infrastructure and security

D) Enhanced performance monitoring capabilities

277.   What is a potential consequence of vendor lock-in in cloud computing?

A) Enhanced flexibility in contract negotiations

B) Decreased data portability

C) Increased options for data migration

D) Improved scalability of resources

278.   What is one risk associated with personnel threats in cloud computing?

A) Loss of data due to natural disasters

B) Unauthorized access to sensitive information

C) Decreased regulatory compliance

D) Limited scalability of resources

279. What risk is magnified by cloud computing, particularly concerning internal personnel and remote access?

A) Data loss

B) Unauthorized disclosure

C) Vendor lock-in

D) Network outages

280. Why cannot the ire legal liability for breaches of Personally Identifiable Information (PII) be transferred to the cloud provider?

A) Due to contractual limitations

B) Because of regulatory compliance requirements

C) Because cloud providers are not legally responsible

D) Due to limitations in technology

281. What are some potential adverse results from breaches in cloud computing that should be addressed in the Business Impact Analysis (BIA)?

A) Increased customer trust

B) Loss of competitive advantage

C) Enhanced goodwill

D) Decreased contractual obligations

282.   Why must the BIAO consider vendor lock-in/lock-out risks for operations migrated to the cloud?

A) To ensure regulatory compliance

B) To address potential legal repercussions

C) To mitigate the impact of unauthorized disclosure

D) To evaluate the long-term implications of cloud migration

283.   What aspects should be addressed in negotiations between the cloud customer and provider regarding Business Continuity/Disaster Recovery (BC/DR)?

A) Service needs and policy enforcement only

B) BC/DR planning and execution responsibilities

C) Audit capabilities and security measures

D) Service level agreements and uptime guarantees

284.   What are the three general means of using cloud backups for Business Continuity/Disaster Recovery (BC/DR)?

A) On-premises backup, cloud backup, and third-party backup

B) Replicated data, third-party cloud backup, and private architecture backup

C) Private architecture backup, cloud service as backup, and cloud provider as backup

D) Cloud-to-cloud backup, hybrid backup, and offsite backup

285.   What factors should be considered in negotiations with cloud providers if the organization maintains its own IT enterprise and uses a cloud provider as a backup?

A) Frequency of backups and audit capabilities

B) Security of the data and systems and ISP costs

C) Monthly caps on upload bandwidth and service level agreements

D) Availability of third-party backups and legal compliance

286.   What is the primary concern in all aspects related to security practices, especially during disaster situations?

A) Financial implications

B) Legal compliance

C) Health and human safety

D) Regulatory requirements

287.   Why is failover testing necessary for Business Continuity/Disaster Recovery (BC/DR) plans?

A) To ensure legal compliance

B) To identify vulnerabilities in the backup systems

C) To minimize the risk of data breaches

D) To fulfill statutory requirements

288.   What is the recommended frequency for Business Continuity/Disaster Recovery (BC/DR) testing according to industry guidance?

A) Monthly

B) Quarterly

C) Annually

D) Biennially

289. What should be coordinated well with the cloud provider before conducting Business Continuity/Disaster Recovery (BC/DR) testing?

A) Failover procedures

B) Data backup schedules

C) Testing Schedule

D) Liability for problems incurred during testing

290. What should be explicitly detailed in the contract between the customer and cloud provider regarding failover and return to normal operations?

A) Failover frequency

B) Emergency contacts

C) Timeframe for failover after notice

D) Testing frequency

291. Which aspect of cloud operations might be at little or no additional cost if offered as part of the standard cloud service?

A) Security measures

B) Audit capabilities

C) Disaster recovery backup

D) Failover procedures

292. What is the purpose of failover testing in Business Continuity/Disaster Recovery (BC/DR) planning?

A) To simulate a disaster event

B) To train personnel in emergency response

C) To identify vulnerabilities in backup systems

D) To establish communication protocols

293.   Which risk is highlighted as being magnified by cloud computing?

A) Unauthorized disclosure

B) Data security

C) Internal communication

D) Vendor lock-in

294.   Why cannot the entire legal liability for Personally Identifiable Information (PII) breaches be shifted to the cloud provider?

A) Due to regulatory restrictions

B) Because of contractual limitations

C) Cloud providers are not legally responsible

D) Limitations in technology

295.   What aspects should be discussed in negotiations between the cloud customer and provider regarding Business Continuity/Disaster Recovery (BC/DR)?

A) Service needs and policy enforcement only

B) BC/DR planning and execution responsibilities

C) Audit capabilities and security measures

D) Service level agreements and uptime guarantees

296.   What are the three general means of using cloud backups for Business Continuity/Disaster Recovery (BC/DR)?

A) On-premises backup, cloud backup, and third-party backup

B) Replicated data, third-party cloud backup, and private architecture backup

C) Private architecture backup, cloud service as backup, and cloud provider as backup

D) Cloud-to-cloud backup, hybrid backup, and offsite backup

297.   What factors should be considered in negotiations with cloud providers if the organization maintains its IT enterprise and uses a cloud provider as a backup?

A) Frequency of backups and audit capabilities

B) Security of the data and systems and ISP costs

C) Monthly caps on upload bandwidth and service level agreements

D) Availability of third-party backups and legal compliance

298.   What is the term we use to describe the general ease and efficiency of moving data from one cloud provider either to another cloud provider or down from the cloud?

A) Mobility

B) Elasticity

C) Obfuscation

D) Portability

299.   Countermeasures for protecting cloud operations against external attackers include all of the following, except:

A) Continual monitoring for anomalous activity

B) Detailed and extensive background checks

C) Hardened devices and systems, including servers, hosts, hypervisors, and virtual machines

D) Regular and detailed configuration/change management activities

300.   All of the following are techniques to enhance the portability of cloud data to minimize the potential of vendor lock-in except:

A) Avoid proprietary data formats

B) Use DRM and DLP solutions widely throughout the cloud operation

C) Ensure there are no physical limitations to moving

D) Ensure favorable contract terms to support portability

301.   Which of the following is a technique used to attenuate risks to the cloud environment, resulting in loss or theft of a device used for remote access?

A) Remote kill switch

B) Dual control

C) Muddling

D) Safe harbor

302.   Each of the following are dependencies that must be considered when reviewing the BIA after cloud migration:

A) The cloud provider's suppliers

B) The cloud provider's vendors

C) The cloud provider's utilities

D) The cloud provider's resellers

303.   When reviewing the BIA after a cloud migration, the organization should consider new factors related to data breach impacts. One of these new factors is:

A) Legal liability cannot be transferred to the cloud provider.

B) Many states have data breach notification laws.

C) Breaches can cause the loss of proprietary data.

D) Breaches can cause the loss of intellectual property.

304.   The cloud customer will have the most control of their data and systems, and the cloud provider will have the least amount of responsibility, in which cloud computing arrangement?

A) IaaS

B) PaaS

C) SaaS

D) Community cloud

305.   After a cloud migration, the BIA should be updated to include a review of the new risks and impacts associated with cloud operations; this review should include an analysis of the possibility of vendor lock-in/lock-out. This risk analysis may not have to be performed as a new effort because a lot of the material that would be included is already available from which of the following?

A) NIST

B) The cloud provider

C) The cost-benefit analysis the organization conducted when deciding on cloud migration

D) Open-source providers

306.   A poorly negotiated cloud service contract could result in ale following detrimental effects:

A) Vendor lock-in

B) Malware

C) Unfavorable terms

D) Lack of necessary services

307.   Because of multitenancy, specific risks in the public cloud that do not exist in the other cloud service models include all the following except:

A) Risk of loss/disclosure due to legal seizures

B) Information bleed

C) DoS/DDoS

D) Escalation of privilege

308.   Countermeasures for protecting cloud operations against internal threats include all of the following except:

A) Active physical surveillance and monitoring

B) Active electronic surveillance and monitoring

C) Redundant ISPs

D) Masking and obfuscation of data for all personnel without the need to know for raw data

309.	Countermeasures for protecting cloud operations against internal threats include all of the following:

A) Broad contractual protections to ensure the provider is ensuring an extreme level of trust in its personnel

B) Financial penalties for the cloud provider in the event of negligence or malice on the part of its personnel

C) DLP solutions

D) Scalability

310. Countermeasures for protecting cloud operations against internal threats include all of the following:

A) Separation of duties

B) Least privilege

C) Conflict of interest

D) Mandatory vacation

311. Benefits for addressing BC/DR offered by cloud operations include all of the following, except:

A) Metered service

B) Distributed, remote processing, and storage of data

C) Fast replication

D) Regular backups offered by cloud providers

312. All of the following methods can be used to attenuate the harm caused by escalation of privilege except:

A) Extensive access control and authentication tools and techniques

B) Analysis and review of all log data by trained, skilled personnel on the frequent and effective use of cryptographic sanitization tools

C) The use of automated analysis tools such as SIM, SIEM, and SEM solutions

313. What is the hypervisor malicious attackers would prefer to attack?

A) Type 1

B) Type 2

C) Type 3

D) Type 4

314. What is the term used to describe the loss of access to data because the cloud provider has ceased operation?

A) Closing

B) Vendor lock-out

C) Vendor lock-in

D) Masking

315. Because PaaS implementations are so often used for software development, what is one of the vulnerabilities that should always be kept in mind?

A) Malware

B) Loss/theft of portable devices

C) Backdoors

D) DoS/DDoS

316. What is the primary objective of domains called "Responsibilities in the Cloud"?

A) To explore various cloud computing platforms

B) To discuss the importance of data encryption in cloud computing

C) To examine the roles and responsibilities of cloud customers and providers

D) To analyze the impact of cloud computing on financial investments

317. What is one of cloud customers' main challenges?

A) Lack of access to cloud infrastructure

B) Limited control over data storage and processing

C) Inability to negotiate contract terms with cloud vendors

D) Difficulty in selecting secure software for cloud deployment

318. In cloud computing, what does the term "SLA" stand for?

A) Service Level Agreement

B) Security and Liability Agreement

C) System Lifecycle Assessment

D) Software Licensing Agreement

319. What analogy does the text use to describe the relationship between a cloud customer and vendor?

A) Landlord and tenant

B) Buyer and seller

C) Investor and broker

D) Teacher and student

320.   What aspect of cloud computing does the financial investment analogy highlight?

A) Lack of regulatory oversight

B) Difficulty in selecting suitable service providers

C) Responsibility for protecting client assets

D) Volatility of investment returns

321. What role does the cloud customer play in protecting Personally Identifiable Information (PII)?

A) They have complete control over data storage and processing.

B) They are responsible for legal compliance but lack control over security measures.

C) They delegate all security responsibilities to the cloud vendor.

D) They have physical access to the data centers where information is stored.

322.   What does the text suggest is a significant challenge in cloud computing?

A) Lack of available case law

B) Overabundance of regulatory oversight

C) Rapidly evolving security standards

D) Excessive government intervention

323.   Which aspect of cloud computing is described as "unnatural" in the text?

A) Customer liability for regulatory infractions

B) Lack of physical access to data centers

C) Dependency on third-party security measures

D) Inability to mandate security controls

324.   What is the primary focus of cloud customers?

A) Maximizing computing capabilities

B) Minimizing contractual obligations

C) Reducing costs and increasing productivity

D) Ensuring complete control over data storage

325.   Which regulatory framework is mentioned as applicable to cloud data centers processing medical information?

A) HIPAA

B) PCI DSS

C) GDPR

D) FISMA

326.   In an Infrastructure as a Service (IaaS) model, what is the primary responsibility of the cloud provider?

A) Securing the entire infrastructure

B) Installing and configuring software applications

C) Managing access controls for data storage

D) Ensuring compliance with regulatory standards

327.   What is a characteristic feature of a honeypot in cloud security?

A) It contains valuable data to attract attackers.

B) It serves as a primary access point for cloud users.

C) It encrypts all incoming and outgoing network traffic.

D) It relies on intrusion prevention systems for protection.

328.   What is the purpose of a firewall in cloud computing?

A) To detect zero-day exploits

B) To monitor network traffic

C) To prevent unauthorized access

D) To manage virtualized environments

329.   How do virtual private networks enhance cloud security?

A) By encrypting data in transit

B) By detecting malicious activity

C) By blocking unauthorized users

D) By isolating network segments

330.   What is the primary responsibility of the cloud customer in a
        Software as a Service (SaaS) model?

A) Managing physical security

B) Installing and securing applications

C) Configuring virtualized environments

D) Monitoring network traffic

331. What role does the management plane play in cloud data center operations?

A) Monitoring physical security measures

B) Controlling access to network resources

C) Managing hardware and software configurations

D) Auditing compliance with regulatory standards

332. How does a vulnerability assessment differ from an Intrusion Detection System (IDS)?

A) A vulnerability assessment focuses on known vulnerabilities, while an IDS detects abnormal behavior.

B) A vulnerability assessment detects zero-day exploits, while an IDS scans for outdated software.

C) A vulnerability assessment relies on behavior-based algorithms, while an IDS uses defined rule sets.

D) A vulnerability assessment prevents unauthorized access, while an IDS monitors network traffic.

333. What is a crucial consideration for cloud providers when selecting the location of a data center?

A) Proximity to competitors' facilities

B) Accessibility to urban areas

C) Availability of skilled personnel

D) Exposure to natural disasters

334. How does a cloud provider ensure secure remote administrative access to hardware?

A) By implementing strong authentication measures

B) By restricting physical access to data centers

C) By encrypting data during transmission

D) By deploying intrusion prevention systems

335. What is the purpose of configuring hardware components with secure BIOS settings in a cloud data center?

A) To prevent unauthorized access to virtual machines

B) To ensure compatibility with virtualization management toolsets

C) To facilitate encryption of data at rest

D) To protect against malicious attacks on the hypervisor

336. What responsibility does the cloud provider assume for security in a Platform as a Service (PaaS) model?

A) Securing physical infrastructure

B) Configuring virtualized environments

C) Installing and maintaining operating systems

D) Managing access controls for data storage

337. How does a cloud provider manage the physical plant of a data center?

A) By encrypting data during transmission

B) By implementing firewalls and IDS

C) By controlling access to the facility

D) By monitoring network traffic for anomalies

338.   What is a shared responsibility between cloud customers and providers in securing Infrastructure as a Service (IaaS)?

A) Configuring virtualized environments

B) Securing physical server hardware

C) Managing access controls for data storage

D) Installing and maintaining operating systems

339.   What is the main objective of cloud application security?

A) To introduce readers to cloud computing architecture.

B) To explore the challenges of application design and architecture for the cloud.

C) To discuss network security controls in a cloud environment.

D) To provide an overview of cloud infrastructure management.

340.   In Cloud Application Security, which domain focuses on understanding security concepts relevant to cloud computing?

A) Domain 1: Architectural Concepts and Design Requirements

B) Domain 2: Cloud Data Security

C) Domain 3: Cloud Platform and Infrastructure Security

D) Domain 4: Cloud Application Security

341. What is emphasized as a crucial aspect before migrating applications to the cloud?

A) Ensuring compatibility with legacy systems

B) Evaluating sensitivity characteristics of data

C) Implementing advanced encryption techniques

D) Maximizing resource sharing with other cloud tenants

342. What is the ultimate responsibility emphasized regarding data ownership in cloud computing?

A) Cloud service provider responsibility

B) Shared responsibility between provider and customer

C) Responsibility for the organization's IT department

D) Sole responsibility of the data owner

343. What term is used to describe the process of moving an existing legacy enterprise application to the cloud with minimal code changes?

A) Cloud migration

B) Application modernization

C) Forklifting

D) Hybridization

344. What is identified as a potential risk associated with open-source libraries in cloud applications?

A) Limited customization options

VERSAtile Reads

B) Reduced scalability

C) Higher susceptibility to tampering

D) Increased licensing costs

345.   What challenges do developers often face when working in a new cloud environment?

A) Lack of available documentation

B) Overabundance of security tools

C) Familiarity with existing infrastructure

D) Simplified development processes

346.   Which organization publishes reports on Cloud Computing's Top Threats, such as "The Treacherous 12"?

A) Cloud Security Alliance (CSA)

B) Open Web Application Security Project (OWASP)

C) International Organization for Standardization (ISO)

D) National Institute of Standards and Technology (NIST)

347.   What characteristic of cloud computing introduces complexities for developers and administrators?

A) Standardization of deployment models

B) Limitations on third-party administrators

C) Multitenancy and resource sharing

D) Simplified service models

348. Which phase of the Cloud Secure Software Development Life Cycle (SDLC) focuses on identifying the business needs of the application?

A) Defining

B) Designing

C) Development

D) Testing

349. What is a primary consideration during the disposal phase of the software development life cycle?

A) Updating application features

B) Ensuring data security

C) Extending application support

D) Improving user experience

350. Which ISO/IEC standard provides guidelines for secure application development?

A) ISO/IEC 27001

B) ISO/IEC 27034-1

C) ISO/IEC 27002

D) ISO/IEC 27005

351. What is the primary focus of identity and Access Management (IAM) in cloud computing?

A) Ensuring network connectivity

B) Managing user credentials and permissions

C) Optimizing cloud resource allocation

D) Securing physical infrastructure

352.   What component of IAM is responsible for establishing a user's identity?

A) Policy Management

B) Authentication

C) Federation

D) Identity Repositories

353.   In the context of cloud application deployment, what is a common challenge related to on-premise applications?

A) Inadequate security measures

B) Dependency on cloud infrastructure

C) Difficulty in provisioning user accounts

D) Performance degradation due to remote calls

354.   What is a crucial aspect of access management in the IAM process?

A) Provisioning unique identity assertions

B) Implementing role-based access controls

C) Enforcing strict password policies

D) Establishing cross-organizational trust

355.   What is the key role of the federation in identity and access management?

A) Managing user authentication

B) Facilitating information exchange between organizations

C) Storing user credentials securely

D) Enforcing access control policies

356. Which phase of the Cloud Secure Software Development Life Cycle (SDLC) involves developing user stories and interface designs?

A) Defining

B) Designing

C) Development

D) Testing

357. What is the primary purpose of access management in cloud computing?

A) To allocate physical resources

B) To enforce network segmentation

C) To control user access to resources

D) To optimize data storage efficiency

358. How does the Cloud Security Alliance contribute to cloud computing security?

A) By developing cloud-based software tools

B) By publishing reports on cloud computing threats

C) By providing cloud infrastructure services

D) By conducting penetration testing for cloud applications

359. Which component of IAM is responsible for enforcing access control policies based on business requirements?

A) Authentication

B) Authorization

C) Policy Management

D) Identity Repositories

360. What distinguishes the cloud-secure SDLC from the traditional SDLC?

A) Inclusion of the disposal phase

B) Emphasis on network security

C) Reduced focus on user training

D) Greater reliance on proprietary software

361. What challenges do developers face when migrating on-premise applications to the cloud?

A) Loss of data integrity

B) Incompatibility with cloud infrastructure

C) Increased reliance on proprietary libraries

D) Difficulty in provisioning user roles

362. What is the purpose of the Treacherous 12 report published by the Cloud Security Alliance?

A) To outline best practices for cloud migration

Practice Questions

VERSAtile Reads

B) To identify common pitfalls in cloud application development

C) To highlight top cloud computing threats

D) To promote collaboration among cloud service providers

363. What phase of the Cloud Secure Software Development Life Cycle (SDLC) involves vulnerability scanning and penetration testing?

A) Defining

B) Designing

C) Development

D) Testing

364. What is the primary objective of ISO/IEC 27034-1 standards for secure application development?

A) To provide guidelines for hardware procurement

B) To establish protocols for network encryption

C) To define best practices for software development

D) To ensure compliance with data protection regulations

365. Which component of IAM is responsible for managing user roles and permissions?

A) Authentication

B) Authorization

C) Policy Management

D) Identity Repositories

366.   What is a critical consideration when deploying cloud applications that rely on APIs?

A) Ensuring compatibility with legacy systems

B) Validating the trustworthiness of APIs

C) Minimizing reliance on third-party administrators

D) Enhancing encryption techniques for data transmission

367.   What is a potential risk associated with poor documentation in cloud application development?

A) Increased deployment efficiency

B) Improved user experience

C) Reduced scalability

D) Enhanced security posture

368.   Which component of IAM is responsible for verifying the identity of users and devices?

A) Authentication

B) Authorization

C) Policy Management

D) Identity Repositories

369.   Which one of the following is the superior benefit of an external audit?
A) Independence
B) Oversight
C) Cheaper
D) Better results

370.   In audit practices, which one is the law resulted from a lack of independence?

A) HIPAA

B) GLBA

C) SOX

D) ISO 27064

371. Which one of the following are the obsolete report types?

A) SAS 70

B) SSAE 16

C) SOC 1

D) SOC 3

372.   Which one of the following is the most aligned report with financial control audits?

A) SOC 1

B) SOC 2

C) SOC 3

D) SSAE 16

373.   What is the objective of a SOC 3 report?

A) Absolute assurances

B) Compliance with PCI/DSS

C) HIPAA compliance

D) Seal of approval

374.   What is the objective of gap analysis performance?

A)   To begin the benchmarking process

B)   To provide assurances to cloud customers

C)   To ensure proper accounting practices are being used

D)   To ensure all controls are in place and working properly

375.   Which organizations are created and maintained by the GAAPs?

A)   ISO

B)   ISO/IEC

C)   PCI Council

D)   AICPA

376.   In the financial industry, which law addresses security and privacy matters?

A)   GLBA

B)   FERPA

C)   SOX

D)   HIPAA

377.   Which one of the followings is not the example of a highly regulated environment?

A)   Healthcare

B)   Financial services

C) Wholesale or distribution

D) Public companies

378. Which one of the followings is the SOC report subtypes addressing a point in time?

A) SOC 2

B) Type I

C) Type II

D) SOC 3

379. Which one of the SOC report subtypes spans a period?

A) SOC 2

B) SOC 3

C) SOC 1

D) Type II

380. Which of the followings refers to the right to be forgotten?

A) The right to no longer pay taxes

B) Erasing criminal history

C) The right to have all of a data owner's data erased

D) Masking

381. Which of the following documents should be a part of a right to audit?

A) SLA

B) PLA

C) All cloud providers

D) Masking

382. Which of the following was enacted by the SOX?

A) Poor BOD oversight

B) Lack of independent audits

C) Poor financial controls

D) All of the above

383. Identify the component of GLBA.

A) The right to be forgotten

B) EU Data Directives

C) The information security program

D) The right to audit

384. Which one of the following is not related to the HIPAA controls?

A) Administrative controls

B) Technical controls

C) Physical controls

D) Financial controls

385. What does the doctrine of the proper law refer to?

A) How jurisdictional disputes are settled

B) The law that is applied after the first law is applied

C) The determination of what law will apply to a case

D) The proper handling of eDiscovery materials

386.   Which of the following refers to the Restatement (Second) Conflict of Law?

A) The basis for deciding which laws are most appropriate in a situation where conflicting laws exist

B) When judges restate the law in an opinion

C) How jurisdictional disputes are settled

D) Whether local or federal laws apply in a situation

387.   What are the characteristics of the Stored Communications Act (SCA)?

A) It is old

B) It is in bad need of updating

C) It is unclear about current technologies

D) All of the above

388.   Which one of the following is the lowest level of the CSA STAR program?

A) Continuous monitoring

B) Self-assessment

C) Hybridization

D) Attestation

389. Which one of the following is a valid risk management metric?

A) KPI

B) KRI

C) SLA

D) SOC

390. Which frameworks focus on design implementation and management?

A) ISO 31000:2009

B) HIPAA

C) ISO 27017

D) NIST 800-92

391. Which frameworks find the top eight security risks based on likelihood and impact?

A) NIST 800-53

B) ISO 27000

C) ENISA

D) COBIT

392. Identify the levels of the CSA STAR program.

A) Self-assessment

B) Third-party assessment-based certification

C) SOC 2 audit certification

D) Continuous monitoring–based certification

393. Which ISO standard addresses the security risk in a supply chain?

A) ISO 27001

B) ISO/IEC 28000:2007

C) ISO 18799

D) ISO 31000:2009

394. Identify risk management frameworks.

A) NIST SP 800-37

B) European Union Agency for Network and Information Security (ENISA)

C) Key risk indicators (KRI)

D) ISO 31000:2009

395. Which one of the following is the best defined risk?

A) Threat coupled with a breach

B) Vulnerability coupled with an attack

C) Threat coupled with a threat actor

D) Threat coupled with a vulnerability

396. Which one of the following is not a component of the ENISA Top 8 Security Risks of cloud computing?

A) Vendor lock-in

B) Isolation failure

C) Insecure or incomplete data deletion

D) Availability

397. Which one of the followings is a risk management way that halts a business function?

A) Mitigation

B) Acceptance

C) Transference

D) Avoidance

398. Which one of the following is best to describe a cloud carrier?

A) A person or entity responsible for making a cloud service available to consumers

B) The intermediary who provides connectivity and transport of cloud services between cloud providers and cloud consumers

C) The person or entity responsible for keeping cloud services running for customers

D) The person or entity responsible for transporting data across the Internet

399. Which method of risk is associated with insurance?

A) Transference

B) Avoidance

C) Acceptance

D) Mitigation

400. Which of the following components are part of a CCSP and should be reviewed when looking at contracting with a cloud service provider?

A) The physical layout of the datacenter

B) Background checks for the provider's personnel

C) Use of subcontractors

D) Redundant uplink grafts

Answers

1.   B) Programming as a Service

Explanation: Programming as a Service is not a standard cloud service model. The standard models are Software as a Service (SaaS), Infrastructure as a Service (IaaS), and Platform as a Service (PaaS).

2.   D) Smart hubs

Explanation: Smart hubs have not yet directly contributed to the advancement of cloud services' viability. The other options, such as virtualization, widely available broadband, and cryptographic connectivity, have played significant roles in enabling cloud computing.

3.   A) SLAs

Explanation: Cloud vendors are held to contractual obligations with specified metrics through Service Level Agreements (SLAs).

4.   C) Business requirements

Explanation: Business requirements drive security decisions in cloud computing, as organizations are required to align security measures with their specific operational needs.

5.   D) Availability

Explanation: If a cloud customer cannot access the cloud provider, it affects the availability aspect of the CIA triad, which refers to ensuring that systems and data are available when needed.

6.   D) Key escrow

Explanation: Cloud Access Security Brokers (CASBs) typically offer services related to Single Sign-On (SSO), Business Continuity/Disaster Recovery/Continuity of Operations Planning (BC/DR/COOP), and Identity and Access Management (IAM), but not typically critical escrow services.

7.   D) Magnetic swipe cards

Explanation: Encryption can be used in various aspects of cloud computing, including storage, remote access, and secure sessions, but not with magnetic swipe cards.

8.   B) Eliminating risks

Explanation: Cloud migration may offer various benefits, including reduced personnel costs, operational expenses, and increased efficiency. However, it does not eliminate risks; instead, it shifts a few risks from the organization to the cloud provider.

9.   B) Negating the need for backups

Explanation: While the generally accepted definition of cloud computing characteristics such as on-demand services, resource pooling, and measured or metered service, it does not negate the need for backups. Backups remain crucial in cloud computing for ensuring data protection.

10.   D) Insufficient bandwidth

Explanation: Vendor lock-in can occur due to unfavorable contracts, statutory compliance requirements, and proprietary data formats. Insufficient bandwidth may affect performance but is not directly related to vendor lock-in.

11.   B) Vendor lock-out

Explanation: The risk that a cloud provider might go out of business and the cloud customer might not be able to recover data is known as vendor lock-out.

12.   B) Reversed charging configuration

Explanation: Broad network access, rapid scaling, and on-demand self-service are all features of cloud computing, but a reversed charging configuration is not a characteristic feature.

13.   C) Cloud customer

Explanation: Ultimately, the responsibility for the security of Personally Identifiable Information (PII) uploaded to a cloud provider lies with the customer.

14.   B) BIA

Explanation: Business Impact Analysis (BIA) determines an organization's critical paths, processes, and assets, helping in disaster recovery and business continuity planning.

15.   A) Private

Explanation: The cloud deployment model featuring organizational ownership of hardware and infrastructure and usage restricted to members of that organization is known as a private cloud.

16.   B) Public

Explanation: The cloud deployment model, characterized by ownership by a cloud provider and services offered to anyone who wants to subscribe, is known as a public cloud.

17.   D) Community

Explanation: The cloud deployment model featuring joint ownership of assets among an affinity group is known as a community cloud.

18.   B) PaaS

Explanation: Platform as a Service (PaaS) allows customers to install their software and operating systems on vendor-provided hardware, making it suitable for software development and testing.

19.   C) SaaS

Explanation: Software as a Service (SaaS) provides a fully operational environment with minimal maintenance or administration necessary, making it suitable for organizations that want ready-to-use applications.

20.   A) IaaS

Explanation: Infrastructure as a Service (IaaS) provides a bare-bones environment where customers can replicate their enterprise for Business Continuity/Disaster Recovery (BC/DR) purposes, as it offers virtualized computing resources.

21.   B) Broad network access, on-demand services, resource pooling, measured service

Explanation: According to the NIST definition, critical characteristics of cloud computing include broad network access, on-demand self-service, resource pooling, and measured service.

22.   A) Infrastructure as a Service (IaaS)

Explanation: Infrastructure as a Service (IaaS) allows customers to install their software and operating systems on vendor-provided hardware.

23. B) The ability to allocate resources as needed for immediate usage

Explanation: Elasticity in cloud computing refers to allocating resources as needed, allowing organizations to scale up or down based on demand.

24. C) Community Cloud

Explanation: The cloud deployment model involving resources owned and operated by an affinity group for joint tasks and functions is a community cloud.

25. C) Cloud Service Provider (CSP)

Explanation: In the Software as a Service (SaaS) model, the CSP provider is responsible for administering, patching, and updating software.

26. B) Reduction in operational costs

Explanation: The primary driver pushing organizations toward cloud migration is often the reduction in operational costs associated with cloud services.

27. C) Collecting financial records

Explanation: Gathering business requirements by collecting financial records involves understanding the organization's financial aspects and performance metrics.

28. C) Managing cloud computing infrastructure and deployment

Explanation: The role of a Cloud Architect involves managing cloud computing infrastructure and deployment to ensure optimal performance and efficiency.

29.   B) Platform as a Service (PaaS)

Explanation: Platform as a Service (PaaS) includes everything in Infrastructure as a Service (IaaS), plus operating systems, allowing developers to build, deploy, and manage applications without dealing with the underlying infrastructure.

30.   C) Augmenting internal data center capabilities with managed services during times of increased demand

Explanation: Cloud bursting refers to seamlessly augmenting internal data center capabilities with managed services from a cloud provider during periods of high demand.

31.   C) Fixed resource pooling

Explanation: According to the NIST definition, fixed resource pooling is not essential to cloud computing. Instead, dynamic resource pooling is emphasized, where resources are allocated and reassigned according to demand.

32.   D) Ensuring compliance with regulatory frameworks

Explanation: The primary function of a Cloud Access Security Broker (CASB) is to ensure compliance with regulatory frameworks and security policies while enabling secure cloud adoption.

33.   B) Private Cloud

Explanation: A private cloud deployment model is exclusively owned and operated by a specific organization, providing dedicated resources for their use.

34.   D) To identify critical paths and single points of failure within an organization

Explanation: A business impact analysis (BIA) aims to identify critical paths, processes, and single points of failure within an organization to mitigate risks and ensure business continuity.

35.   A) Infrastructure as a Service (IaaS)

Explanation: In the Infrastructure as a Service (IaaS) model, the customer administers all logical resources, including software and operating systems. At the same time, the cloud provider manages the underlying infrastructure.

36.   C) Reduction in personnel costs

Explanation: One of the primary benefits of cloud migration is the reduction in personnel costs, as organizations can leverage the expertise and resources of cloud providers rather than maintaining sizeable in-house IT teams.

37.   C) Interviewing senior management

Explanation: Gathering business requirements by interviewing senior management involves understanding the organization's strategic goals, objectives, and high-level priorities.

38.   C) Software as a Service (SaaS)

Explanation: In the Software as a Service (SaaS) model, the customer only uploads and processes data on a complete production environment hosted by the provider without managing underlying infrastructure or platforms.

39.   B) Cloud backup

Explanation: Using a cloud-based service for data archival and disaster recovery is commonly called cloud backup.

40.   C) Analyzing network traffic

Explanation: Analyzing traffic is not typically mentioned for gathering business requirements.

41.   B) Ensuring compliance with regulatory frameworks

Explanation: The primary responsibility of regulators in cloud computing is to ensure compliance with regulatory frameworks and security standards to protect user data and privacy.

42.   D) Hybrid Cloud

Explanation: The hybrid cloud deployment model combines elements of both public and private clouds, allowing organizations to leverage both benefits while addressing specific business needs.

43.   C) Providing infrastructure and processing for cloud environments

Explanation: The primary purpose of a Cloud Service Provider (CSP) is to provide infrastructure and processing capabilities for cloud environments, offering services such as computing, storage, and networking.

44.   A) Infrastructure as a Service (IaaS)

Explanation: Infrastructure as a Service (IaaS) offers the highest level of control to the cloud customer, allowing them to manage and control virtualized computing resources, including servers, storage, and networking.

45.   B) Enhanced control over data security

Explanation: The main advantage of using a Cloud Access Security Broker (CASB) is enhanced control over data security, including visibility, policy enforcement, and threat protection across multiple cloud services.

46.   C) The ease of using and administering cloud services

Explanation: "Simplicity" in cloud computing refers to the ease of using and administering cloud services, enabling users to access and manage resources with minimal complexity.

47.   C) Software as a Service (SaaS)

Explanation: In the Software as a Service (SaaS) model, the cloud provider is responsible for administering software applications and hardware resources. At the same time, customers access them via the internet.

48.   D) Identifying critical paths and single points of failure within an organization

Explanation: A Business Impact Analysis (BIA) primarily identifies critical paths, processes, and single points of failure within an organization to assess the potential impact of disruptions and prioritize recovery efforts.

49.   C) Resource pooling

Explanation: Resource pooling allows customers to scale their computing and storage needs with little or no intervention from the provider. This ensures that resources are dynamically allocated and shared among multiple users as needed.

50.   D) A cloud customer leases cloud resources while a cloud user accesses them.

Explanation: A cloud customer typically leases or subscribes to cloud resources or services from a cloud service provider, whereas a cloud user accesses these resources or services the customer provides.

51.   B) Platform as a Service (PaaS)

Explanation: Platform as a Service (PaaS) allows organizations to develop, run, and manage applications without worrying about the underlying infrastructure. This model offers more security control than SaaS because customers control application security configurations.

52.   C) Enhancing control over data security

Explanation: CASBs enhance control over data security by providing visibility, compliance, and threat protection across cloud applications. They act as intermediaries between cloud users and service providers to enforce security policies.

53.   C) Community Cloud

Explanation: Community Cloud is characterized by infrastructure owned and operated by independent organizations for exclusive use by a specific community of users who share common goals, requirements, policies, and compliance considerations.

54.   A) The flexibility of resource allocation

Explanation: Elasticity in cloud computing refers to the ability to dynamically allocate and deallocate resources based on workload demands, providing flexibility and scalability to meet changing requirements.

55.   C) Software as a Service (SaaS)

Explanation: In the Software as a Service (SaaS) model, the provider hosts and manages software applications and underlying infrastructure, allowing users to access the software via the Internet.

56.   D) Providing infrastructure and processing for cloud environments

Explanation: Cloud Service Providers (CSPs) offer infrastructure, platforms, and services necessary for cloud computing, including hardware, networking, storage, and virtualization.

57.   D) Measured service

Explanation: Measured service refers to the characteristic of cloud computing where resource usage is monitored, controlled, and reported, allowing customers to pay for only the resources they use.

58.   C) Flexibility to leverage both private and public cloud resources

Explanation: A hybrid cloud deployment model allows organizations to leverage private and public cloud resources, optimizing workload placement and meeting specific business requirements.

59.   B) To discuss architectural principles in cloud security

Explanation: The primary objective of the chapter "Design Requirements" is to discuss architectural principles and requirements related to cloud security to ensure robust and secure cloud deployments.

60.   A) Conducting a risk assessment

Explanation: Conducting a risk assessment is typically the first step in creating a sound security program, as it helps identify and prioritize potential risks and threats to an organization's assets and operations.

61.   B) To identify critical aspects of the organization

Explanation: The purpose of a Business Impact Analysis (BIA) is to identify critical aspects of the organization, such as processes, systems, and assets, and assess the potential impact of disruptions on business operations.

62.   C) Intellectual property

Explanation: Intellectual property, such as patents, trademarks, and copyrights, is an example of an intangible asset that has value but lacks physical substance.

63.   D) It identifies aspects necessary for the organization's operation

Explanation: Determining criticality in the context of Business Impact Analysis (BIA) helps identify aspects necessary for the organization's operation, ensuring that resources and efforts are focused on protecting essential functions and assets.

64.   A) It is the level of risk that organizations find unacceptable

Explanation: Risk appetite refers to the amount and type of risk an organization is willing to accept or tolerate in pursuit of its objectives. It represents the level of risk that organizations find unacceptable or intolerable.

65. D) Mitigation

Explanation: Mitigation is the primary way for organizations to address risk, involving implementing controls and measures to reduce the likelihood or impact of identified risks.

66. A) Infrastructure as a Service

Explanation: IaaS stands for Infrastructure as a Service, where cloud providers offer virtualized computing resources over the internet, including servers, storage, networking, and other infrastructure components.

67. C) The customer manages all aspects of the environment, including the OS

Explanation: In the Platform as a Service (PaaS) model, the provider offers a platform allowing customers to develop, run, and manage applications while the customer manages the applications and data.

68. A) Implementing physical solid access controls

Explanation: Implementing physical solid access controls is recommended for securing devices in a cloud environment to prevent unauthorized access and protect physical assets.

69. B) It allows data to be processed in the cloud without decryption, preserving the confidentiality

Explanation: Homomorphic encryption allows computations on encrypted data without decrypting it first, preserving data confidentiality while enabling data processing in the cloud.

70.   C) To implement multiple overlapping security measures

Explanation: Layered defenses in cloud security involve implementing multiple security measures at different layers of the IT infrastructure to provide comprehensive protection against various threats and vulnerabilities.

71.   D) Utilizing data loss prevention (DLP) solutions

Explanation: Utilizing data loss prevention (DLP) solutions is a recommended measure for securing BYOD assets accessing the cloud, helping prevent unauthorized access and leakage of sensitive information.

72.   A) Infrastructure as a Service (IaaS)

Explanation: Infrastructure as a Service (IaaS) grants the customer the most responsibility and authority as they control the infrastructure, including virtual machines, storage, and networking.

73.   C) To reduce the attack surface

Explanation: Hardening devices in a cloud environment reduces the attack surface by implementing security measures and configurations to minimize vulnerabilities and potential entry points for attackers.

74.   B) The customer has less control over the hardware infrastructure

Explanation: In the Platform as a Service (PaaS) model compared to the Infrastructure as a Service (IaaS) model, the customer has less control over the hardware infrastructure as the provider manages the underlying hardware.

75.   C) To administer the software and data

Explanation: In the Software as a Service (SaaS) model, the cloud customer administers the software applications and data, including user access, configurations, and customization.

76.   D) It dictates the actions organizations take to mitigate risk

Explanation: Risk appetite dictates organizations' actions to mitigate risk by setting thresholds for acceptable risk levels and guiding decision-making processes related to risk management.

77.   D) To assess critical paths and processes

Explanation: The Business Impact Analysis (BIA) process aims to assess critical paths and processes within an organization to identify dependencies, vulnerabilities, and potential impacts of disruptions.

78.   A) Implementing strict background checks for all personnel

Explanation: Implementing strict background checks for all personnel is a crucial consideration for cloud customers in dealing with risks associated with physical access to data to prevent insider threats and unauthorized access.

79.   C) Land

Explanation: Land is an example of a tangible asset with a physical substance that can be seen and touched.

80.   C) To reduce risks to an acceptable level

Explanation: The primary goal of the risk management process is to reduce risks to an acceptable level by identifying, assessing, and prioritizing risks and implementing measures to mitigate or manage them.

81.   A) Software as a Service (SaaS)

Explanation: SaaS stands for Software as a Service, where cloud providers manage software applications and make them available to users over the internet on a subscription basis.

82.   C) The customer has control over the software applications and data
Explanation: In the SaaS model, the provider manages the infrastructure, including hardware and operating systems, while the customer controls the software applications and data.

83.   B) The provider manages the operating system and hardware, reducing customer responsibilities
Explanation: PaaS allows customers to focus on developing and managing applications without worrying about the underlying infrastructure, as the provider manages the operating system and hardware.

84.   C) Transferring risks to a third party
Explanation: Risk transference involves shifting the risk to another party through insurance or outsourcing certain activities to specialized vendors.

85.   C) To protect data confidentiality and integrity
Explanation: Encryption ensures that data remains confidential and maintains its integrity by encoding it so that only authorized parties can access and understand it.

Answers

86. C) To secure data while it is being transmitted between network devices
Explanation: Encryption in transit ensures that data remains secure while it travels between network devices, preventing unauthorized interception and access.

87. D) It indicates the level of risk that organizations are willing to accept
Explanation: Risk tolerance refers to the degree of risk an organization is willing to accept to pursue its objectives or goals.

88. C) Both the cloud provider and the customer share responsibility for security
Explanation: Shared responsibility means that while the cloud provider is responsible for certain aspects of security (e.g., infrastructure security), the customer is responsible for others (e.g., data protection and access management).

89. A) To identify critical assets within the organization
Explanation: BIA helps identify critical assets, processes, and functions within an organization, allowing prioritization of resources for protection and recovery efforts.

90. C) Non-essential personnel
Explanation: Critical aspects typically refer to tangible and intangible assets and key business processes essential for the organization's operations.

91. C) A weakness that could fail an entire system

Copyright © 2024 VERSAtile Reads. All rights reserved.
This material is protected by copyright, any infringement will be dealt with legal and punitive action. 146

Explanation: A Single Point of Failure is a vulnerability within a system or process that, if exploited, could lead to the failure of the entire system or process.

92.   C) By implementing alternative processes and redundancies
Explanation: Organizations can mitigate SPOFs by introducing redundancy, failover mechanisms, and alternative processes to ensure that if one component fails, another can take over seamlessly.

93.   C) It represents the level of risk that the organization finds tolerable
Explanation: Risk appetite defines the amount and type of risk that an organization is willing to pursue or retain in pursuit of its objectives.

94.   C) Transference
Explanation: Risk transference involves shifting the risk to another party, such as through insurance or contractual agreements.

95.   C) It allows computations to be performed on encrypted data without decrypting it
Explanation: Homomorphic encryption enables computations to be performed on encrypted data without the need for decryption, enhancing data privacy and security in cloud environments.

96.   D) To enhance the security of cloud infrastructure
Explanation: Hardening devices involves configuring them to remove unnecessary services and tighten security settings, reducing the attack surface and enhancing overall security.

97.   C) It provides multiple overlapping security measures

Explanation: Layered defenses involve deploying multiple security measures at different layers of the infrastructure to provide comprehensive protection against various types of threats.

98.   D) Criticality
Explanation: Gathering business requirements helps determine the full inventory, usefulness, and value of organizational assets, but it doesn't directly assess their criticality.

99.   B) Secure acquisition
Explanation: While the BIA provides valuable information for risk analysis, business continuity/disaster recovery planning, and selection of security controls, it is not directly related to secure acquisition.

100.   D) IaaS
Explanation: In the Infrastructure as a Service (IaaS) model, the customer is responsible for managing and maintaining the operating system, applications, data, and runtime environment.

101.   C) PaaS
Explanation: In the Platform as a Service (PaaS) model, the provider manages the underlying infrastructure, including the operating system and hardware, while the customer is responsible for developing, deploying, and maintaining applications.

102.   B) SaaS
Explanation: In the Software as a Service (SaaS) model, the provider manages everything, including the infrastructure, platform, applications, and data. The customer only interacts with the software application and is responsible for their data.

103.   B) Contract

Explanation: The agreement between the cloud customer and provider, including their respective responsibilities and rights, is codified in a contract or service-level agreement (SLA).

104.   D) All of the above

Explanation: Layered defense includes technological, physical, and administrative controls to provide comprehensive security coverage across different aspects of the organization's infrastructure and operations.

105.   A) Access control process

Explanation: Administrative controls, such as access control processes, policies, and procedures.

106.   A) Firewall software

Explanation: Technological controls are security measures that involve the use of technology to protect information systems and data. Firewall software is a technological control because it uses software to monitor and control incoming and outgoing network traffic based on predetermined security rules, thereby protecting the system from unauthorized access.

107.   D) Fences

Explanation: Physical controls are security measures designed to prevent unauthorized physical access to facilities, equipment, and resources. Fences are a physical control because they act as a barrier to restrict and control access to a property or specific area.

108.   D) Profile formatting

Explanation: Encryption

is essential for protecting data at rest (long-term storage) and data in transit (secure sessions/VPN). It can also be used for near-term storage of virtualized images to ensure data security. However, profile formatting typically refers to the layout and presentation of user profile data rather than the actual storage or transmission of sensitive information, making it less relevant for encryption compared to the other options.

109.   E) All of the above

Explanation: Hardening a device involves enhancing its security posture by reducing its attack surface and minimizing potential vulnerabilities. Improving default accounts, closing unused ports, deleting unnecessary services, and strictly controlling administrator access are all essential steps in this process to mitigate security risks and strengthen the device's defenses against unauthorized access and exploitation.

110.   A) Encrypting the OS and B) Updating and patching the system

Explanation: Hardening a device involves enhancing its security posture to reduce vulnerabilities and minimize potential risks. Encrypting the operating system (OS) helps protect data at rest, while updating and patching the system ensures that known vulnerabilities are addressed, thereby strengthening the device's security. Using video cameras and performing thorough personnel background checks are not typically part of the process of hardening a device but may be components of broader security strategies for physical security and personnel security, respectively.

111.   A)Homomorphic

Explanation: Homomorphic encryption is a cryptographic technique that allows mathematical operations to be performed on encrypted data without decrypting it first. This capability enables computations to be conducted on sensitive data while it remains encrypted, preserving privacy and security.

Answers

VERSAtile Reads

112.   B) Senior Management

Explanation: Risk appetite refers to the level of risk that an organization is willing to accept or tolerate in pursuit of its objectives. Senior management, including executives and top leadership, is primarily responsible for setting the organization's risk appetite based on its strategic goals, values, and risk tolerance. While legislative mandates and contractual agreements may influence risk management practices, they do not directly determine an organization's risk appetite.

113.   C) Residual

Explanation: The residual risk refers to the level of risk that remains after controls and countermeasures have been implemented to mitigate identified risks. It represents the risk that an organization still faces despite its risk management efforts.

114.   B) Reversal

Explanation: Reversal is not a common way of addressing risk. The typical risk response strategies are acceptance, mitigation, and transfer.

115.   D) Two-person integrity

Explanation: Requiring two-person integrity is not typically considered a measure for protecting data on user devices in a Bring Your Own Device (BYOD) environment. Standard measures include DLP (Data Loss Prevention) agents, local encryption, and Multi-factor authentication.

116.   D) Removing all admin accounts

Explanation: Removing all admin accounts is not a mean of hardening devices. Standard methods include using a firm password policy, removing default passwords, and strictly limiting physical access.

117.   C) The likelihood that a threat will exploit a vulnerability

Explanation: Risk is commonly defined as the likelihood of a threat exploiting a vulnerability, negatively impacting an organization's objectives.

118.   D) Sensitivity

Explanation: The military typically uses the sensitivity model for data classification, where data is categorized based on its level of sensitivity or confidentiality.

119.   B) Jurisdiction

Explanation: The geophysical location of data determines its jurisdiction, which may have implications for data privacy laws and regulations.

120.   C) Source and applicable regulation

Explanation: Data labels may include information about the source of the data and the regulations applicable to its handling and storage.

121.   C) Data Discovery

Explanation: Data discovery is collecting electronic evidence for an investigation or lawsuit.

122.   B) By providing accurate and sufficient information

Explanation: Labels aid in discovering data by providing accurate and sufficient information about the data, facilitating its identification and retrieval.

123. A) Label-Based Discovery

Explanation: Label-based discovery relies heavily on the labels created by data owners to identify and locate specific data within an organization's systems.

124. D) To communicate pertinent concepts

Explanation: The main reason for creating data labels is to communicate pertinent concepts about the data, such as its sensitivity, ownership, and usage restrictions.

125. D) Identifying themselves

Explanation: The primary responsibility of data owners during the Create phase of the data lifecycle is to identify themselves as the individuals or entities responsible for the data.

126. A) Create

Explanation: The phase of the data lifecycle that involves identifying data custodians is the Create phase, where data ownership and custodianship are established.

127. B) Data owner

Explanation: In data ownership, the cloud provider typically acts as a data processor or controller, while the data owner remains responsible for the data stored in the cloud.

128. C) By indicating how data should be handled

Explanation: Labels aid in data security efforts by indicating how data should be handled, including specifying access restrictions, encryption requirements, and other security measures.

129.   C) To understand how data will be used

Explanation: The primary purpose of data categorization is to understand how data will be used within an organization, enabling appropriate security and management practices.

130.   C) Create

Explanation: Data classification typically occurs during the Create phase of the data lifecycle, where data is initially generated, collected, or imported into the organization's systems.

131.   A) Sensitivity

Explanation: The primary trait used for data classification is sensitivity, which determines the protection and handling required for the data.

132.   D) Data encryption method

Explanation: Data labels typically do not include information about the data encryption method used, as this is more related to implementing security controls rather than data classification.

133.   C) By indicating how data should be handled

Explanation: Labels aid in data security efforts by indicating how data should be handled, including specifying access restrictions, encryption requirements, and other security measures.

134.   D) To identify and inventory data

Explanation: The primary purpose of data discovery is to identify and inventory data within an organization's systems, including locating data sources and understanding their characteristics.

135.   A) Jurisdiction-Based Discovery

Explanation: Jurisdiction-based discovery relies on the physical location of data sources or storage points to identify relevant data for discovery purposes.

136.   C) To communicate pertinent concepts

Explanation: The primary purpose of data labeling is to communicate pertinent concepts about the data, such as its sensitivity, ownership, and usage restrictions, to facilitate its management and protection.

137.   D) To properly allocate security resources

Explanation: The main objective of data classification is to properly allocate security resources based on the data's sensitivity, importance, and other attributes.

138.   C) Department head or business unit manager

Explanation: In a cloud computing context, the data owner is typically considered the department head or business unit manager responsible for the data.

139.   C) Manipulating, storing, or moving data

Explanation: The responsibility of a data custodian involves tasks such as manipulating, storing, or moving data according to the policies and guidelines set by the data owner.

140.   C) Create

Explanation: The phase of the data lifecycle primarily concerned with identifying the data owner is the Create phase, where the data is initially generated or collected.

141.   D) To assign data custodians

Explanation: Data categorization aims to assign custodians responsible for managing and protecting the data throughout its lifecycle.

142.   C) To understand how data will be used

Explanation: The primary purpose of data categorization is to understand how data will be used within an organization, enabling appropriate security and management practices.

143.   C) Create

Explanation: Data classification typically occurs during the Create phase of the data lifecycle, where data is initially generated, collected, or imported into the organization's systems.

144.   A) Sensitivity

Explanation: The primary trait used for data classification is sensitivity, which determines the protection and handling required for the data.

145.   D) Data encryption method

Explanation: Data labels typically do not include information about the data encryption method used, as this is more related to implementing security controls rather than data classification.

146.   C) By indicating how data should be handled

Explanation: Labels aid in data security efforts by indicating how data should be handled, including specifying access restrictions, encryption requirements, and other security measures.

147.   D) To identify and inventory data

Explanation: The primary purpose of data discovery is to identify and inventory data within an organization's systems, including locating data sources and understanding their characteristics.

148.   A) Jurisdiction-Based Discovery

Explanation: Jurisdiction-based discovery relies on the physical location of data sources or storage points to identify relevant data for discovery purposes.

149.   C) To communicate pertinent concepts

Explanation: The primary purpose of data labeling is to communicate pertinent concepts about the data, such as its sensitivity, ownership, and usage restrictions, to facilitate its management and protection.

150.   D) To properly allocate security resources

Explanation: The main objective of data classification is to properly allocate security resources based on the data's sensitivity, importance, and other attributes.

151.   C) Department head or business unit manager

Explanation: In a cloud computing context, the data owner is typically considered the department head or business unit manager responsible for the data.

152.   C) Manipulating, storing, or moving data

Explanation: The responsibility of a data custodian involves tasks such as manipulating, storing, or moving data according to the policies and guidelines set by the data owner.

153.   C) To enforce security policies across cloud services

Explanation: CASBs are designed to provide security policy enforcement and governance across multiple cloud services. They act as intermediaries between cloud service consumers and providers, enabling organizations to enforce security policies consistently across different cloud platforms and gain visibility into cloud usage.

154.   B) Biometric authentication

Explanation: Biometric authentication, such as fingerprint or iris scans, provides a high level of security because it relies on the unique physical characteristics of individuals, making it difficult for unauthorized users to gain access even if credentials are compromised.

155.   A) Granting users access only to the data and resources required to perform their job functions

Explanation: The principle of least privilege involves restricting users' access rights to only the minimum levels necessary to perform their job functions. This reduces the risk of unauthorized access and limits the potential impact of security breaches or insider threats.

156.   C) Create

Explanation: The phase of the data lifecycle primarily concerned with identifying the data owner is the "Create" phase, as this is when data is generated or acquired. Ownership is typically established at this point.

157.   B) To create data labels

Explanation: Data categorization aims to create labels or tags that indicate the data's sensitivity, criticality, and other attributes for easier management and protection.

158.   C) Create

Explanation: Data classification occurs primarily in the "Create" phase of the data lifecycle, where data is generated or acquired, and its attributes are determined for classification purposes.

159.   A) Sensitivity

Explanation: The primary trait used for data classification is sensitivity, which refers to the confidentiality or importance of the data to an organization.

160.   D) Data encryption method

Explanation: Data labels typically include information such as handling directions, access limitations, and date of scheduled destruction/disposal. However, specific technical details like the data encryption method are usually not included in data labels, as they are more relevant to security implementation than data classification.

161.   C) By indicating how data should be handled

Explanation: Labels aid in data security efforts by indicating how data should be handled, including specifying access restrictions, encryption requirements, and other security measures.

162.   C) Department head or business unit manager

Explanation: In a cloud computing context, the data owner is typically considered the department head or business unit manager responsible for the data and its usage within the organization.

163.   C) Manipulating, storing, or moving data

Explanation: The responsibility of a data custodian includes tasks related to manipulating, storing, or moving data, ensuring its proper management, security, and compliance with organizational policies and procedures.

164.   D) Metadata-based

Explanation: Metadata-based discovery is a valid method of data discovery, providing insights into data attributes and characteristics. Content-based, user-based, and label-based discovery methods are also commonly used for data discovery.

165.   C) Data value

Explanation: Data labels typically provide metadata associated with data assets to aid in their management and understanding. While data labels commonly include information such as the date data was created, the data owner, and the date of scheduled destruction, they typically do not include the actual value of the data. Data value is a subjective assessment and may vary depending on the context or perspective of different stakeholders, making it less suitable for inclusion in standardized data labels. Therefore, option C is the exception.

166. B) Delivery vendor

Explanation: While data labels typically include information about the source of the data, any handling restrictions, and jurisdictional considerations, they generally do not include details about the delivery vendor. The delivery vendor is more relevant to the procurement or supply chain process rather than directly related to the data itself. Therefore, option B is the exception.

167. D) Multi-factor authentication

Explanation: Data labels typically provide metadata associated with data assets to aid in their management and understanding. Confidentiality level, distribution limitations, and access restrictions are common types of information included in data labels to specify how the data should be handled, shared, and protected. However, Multi-factor authentication is a security mechanism used to verify the identity of users accessing systems or applications rather than metadata associated directly with data labels.

168. D) Refractory iterations

Explanation: Refractory iterations do not represent a recognized mode of data analytics. Real-time analytics, data mining, and agile business intelligence are established modes for analyzing and deriving insights from data.

169. B) The cloud customer

Explanation: In the cloud motif, the data owner is typically the cloud customer responsible for the data and its usage, even though it is stored and processed within the cloud provider's infrastructure.

170.   C) The cloud provider

Explanation: In the cloud motif, the data processor is usually the cloud provider who processes the data on behalf of the cloud customer, adhering to the terms outlined in the service agreement.

171.   A) Foundational policy

Explanation: Every security program and process should have a foundational policy that outlines the organization's fundamental principles, objectives, and guidelines governing security practices.

172.   B) Policy review

Explanation: Policy review ensures that organizational policies are regularly assessed and updated to remain relevant and practical. Including policy maintenance, policy enforcement, and policy adjudication are also essential components of comprehensive policy management.

173.   B) Cryptoshredding

Explanation: Cryptoshredding is a method of data disposal in the cloud that involves rendering data unreadable by securely deleting encryption keys associated with the data. This ensures that even if the data remains in storage, it cannot be accessed or decrypted.

174.   A) Copyright

Explanation: Copyright protects the tangible expression of creative ideas, such as literary works, artistic creations, and software code, from unauthorized copying, distribution, and adaptation.

175.   B) Patent

Explanation: A patent provides intellectual property protection for practical manufacturing innovations, granting the inventor exclusive rights to the invention for a limited period, typically 20 years.

176.   D) Trade secret

Explanation: Trade secret protection applies to valuable information, such as sales leads, formulas, or processes that provide a competitive advantage to a business and are kept confidential. Unlike patents or copyrights, trade secrets do not require registration and last indefinitely as long as the information remains secret.

177.   D) Trade secret

Explanation: A confidential recipe for muffins would typically be protected as a trade secret as long as the owner takes reasonable steps to maintain its secrecy and derives economic value from its confidentiality.

178.   C) Trademark

Explanation: A trademark protects intellectual property for logos, symbols, names, or phrases identifying and distinguishing goods or services in the marketplace.

179.   C) Takedown notice

Explanation: The Digital Millennium Copyright Act (DMCA) includes provisions for takedown notices, which allow copyright holders to request removing infringing content from online platforms. However, these notices have been criticized for their potential for abuse and for placing the burden of proof on the accused to contest the takedown.

180.   B) USPTO

Explanation: The United States Patent and Trademark Office (USPTO) is the federal agency responsible for examining and granting patents for new inventions and discoveries.

181.   C) Dip switch validity

Explanation: DRM tools commonly use support-based licensing, local agent enforcement, and media-present checks to enforce intellectual property rights. Dip switch validity is not a typical method used in DRM.

182.   D) The United States

Explanation: While the United States has privacy laws at the state level and industry-specific regulations, it does not have a comprehensive federal privacy law protecting personal data. However, regions such as Asia, Europe, and South America have countries with overarching federal privacy laws.

183.   B) Automatic self-destruct

Explanation: While DRM solutions may include persistency, automatic expiration, and dynamic policy control, automatic self-destruct is not a standard function. DRM aims to control access to digital content and prevent unauthorized use rather than destroying it automatically.

184.   D). Encryption and decryption

Explanation: Encryption and decryption are essential security aspects that must be maintained when migrating data to the cloud to ensure data confidentiality and integrity.

185.   B) Uniformity in data manipulation procedures

Explanation: The data lifecycle in the cloud and the legacy environment may involve uniformity in data manipulation procedures, ensuring consistency and reliability in handling data throughout its lifecycle.

186.   C) Data categorization and labeling

Explanation: During the Create phase, categorizing and labeling data is crucial for effective organization, governance, and security. Properly classified data enables better control over access, ensures compliance with regulations, and facilitates efficient data management throughout its lifecycle.

187.   B) By using secure encryption methods

Explanation: Secure encryption methods ensure that data remains protected, even if it is accessed or intercepted during transmission or storage. Encrypting data created remotely by users helps safeguard its confidentiality and integrity, mitigating the risk of unauthorized access or data breaches. While multi-factor authentication, restricting data access based on user roles, and employing intrusion detection systems are important security measures in the cloud environment, using secure encryption methods is particularly crucial for protecting data created remotely by users.

188.   C) Data encryption

Explanation: In the Store phase, data is stored in the cloud environment, and ensuring its security is paramount. Data encryption is a critical consideration during this phase to protect sensitive information from unauthorized access or breaches. Encrypting data at rest helps safeguard it from potential threats, ensuring confidentiality and integrity. While data duplication, migration, and compression are also important aspects of data management, data encryption takes precedence in securing data stored in the cloud.

189.   C) Implementing a robust authentication mechanism

Explanation: During the Use phase, data is actively accessed and manipulated within the cloud environment. Implementing a robust authentication mechanisms, such as multi-factor authentication, helps ensure that only authorized users can access the data. This protects against unauthorized access and helps maintain the confidentiality and integrity of the data. While physical access control, data redundancy, and data retention policies are important considerations in overall data security, implementing a robust authentication mechanisms is particularly critical during the Use phase to prevent unauthorized access to sensitive information.

190.   Encryption of shared files and communications

 Explanation: Encryption of shared files and communications is particularly relevant during the Share phase of the cloud data life cycle to protect data confidentiality and prevent unauthorized access to sensitive information.

191.   C) To control the geographic distribution of data

 Explanation: Export restrictions in the Share phase of the cloud data life cycle aim to control the geographic distribution of data to ensure compliance with legal and regulatory requirements regarding data exportation.

192.   B) Greater susceptibility to insider threats

 Explanation: Storing cloud backups in the same environment as production data increases the risk of insider threats because individuals with access to production data may also have backups, potentially leading to unauthorized or malicious activities.

193.   B) Overwriting data with random patterns

VERSAtile Reads

Explanation: Overwriting data with random patterns is recommended for securely erasing data in the Destroy phase of the cloud data life cycle to ensure that the data cannot be recovered or reconstructed.

194.   C) File storage allows direct access to individual data blocks.

Explanation: In cloud storage architectures, file storage allows direct access to individual data blocks, while block storage provides a lower-level interface where data is organized into blocks accessed via block-level protocols.

195.   C) Infrastructure as a Service (IaaS)

Explanation: Volume storage, such as file and block storage, is often associated with Infrastructure as a Service (IaaS) cloud service model, where users can provision and manage storage resources as needed.

196.   D) Data erasure coding

Explanation: Data erasure coding is commonly implemented in volume storage architectures to ensure resilience by distributing data across multiple storage nodes, enabling data recovery even if some nodes fail.

197.   C) Compromised data confidentiality

Explanation: Mismanaged cryptographic keys in cloud data archiving can lead to compromised data confidentiality, as unauthorized parties may gain access to encrypted data if keys are not properly managed and secured.

198.   D) To prevent data degradation and obsolescence

Explanation: It is essential to consider the format of data storage media in long-term archiving in the cloud to prevent data degradation and obsolescence, ensuring that data remains accessible and usable over time.

199.   Background checks for provider staff

Explanation: Background checks for provider staff should be considered when storing data with a third-party provider to ensure that personnel handling sensitive data have undergone appropriate screening and vetting processes.

200.   C) By monitoring data traffic leaving the cloud environment

Explanation: Egress monitoring can benefit data security during the Share phase of the cloud data life cycle by monitoring data traffic leaving the cloud environment, helping to detect and prevent unauthorized data exfiltration or leakage.

201.   C) To ensure compliance with international regulations

Explanation: The primary function of export controls in cloud data sharing is to ensure compliance with international regulations governing data transfer across borders, including restrictions on exporting certain types of data to specific countries or regions.

202.   B) The necessity of segregating production and backup data in the cloud

Explanation: The case of the software repository company highlights the importance of segregating production and backup data in the cloud to prevent the compromise of both sets of data in the event of a security breach or data loss incident.

203.   B) Data integrity

Explanation: Throughout the chapter, data integrity is emphasized as a fundamental concept of data security in cloud data management, ensuring that data remains accurate, consistent, and trustworthy throughout its lifecycle.

204.   C) It protects data from being modified or tampered with.

Explanation: Encryption plays a role in securing data during the Create phase of the cloud data life cycle by protecting data from being modified or tampered with, thereby ensuring its integrity and authenticity.

205.   B) SSL/TLS encryption

Explanation: SSL/TLS encryption is recommended for securing data transmission during the Create phase of the cloud data life cycle to encrypt data in transit and ensure its confidentiality and integrity.

206.   C) Utilizing multi-factor authentication

Explanation: Utilizing multi-factor authentication is a primary consideration for ensuring secure remote access during the Use phase of the cloud data life cycle to enhance authentication security and prevent unauthorized access to cloud resources.

207.   It prevents unauthorized data access.

Explanation: Data owners restricting permissions during the Use phase of the cloud data life cycle is significant as it prevents unauthorized data access, enhancing data security and compliance with access control policies.

208.   A) GDPR (General Data Protection Regulation)

Explanation: The GDPR (General Data Protection Regulation) is mentioned in the text as a consideration for export restrictions during data sharing in the cloud, as it imposes strict rules on transferring personal data outside the European Economic Area.

209.   C) Detecting unauthorized data exfiltration

Explanation: Egress monitoring aims to detect unauthorized data exfiltration in the context of cloud data sharing by monitoring data traffic leaving the cloud environment and identifying any attempts to transfer sensitive data outside the authorized boundaries.

210.   D) Physical and environmental security

Explanation: Physical and environmental security is critical for selecting a storage location during the Archive phase of the cloud data life cycle to ensure that archived data remains protected from physical threats and environmental hazards.

211.   A) To ensure data availability

Explanation: Critical management is crucial during long-term data archiving in the cloud to ensure data availability by effectively managing and preserving archived data over extended periods, preventing data loss or degradation.

212.   D) Retaining data in formats accessible by legacy hardware and software

Explanation: Retaining data in formats accessible by legacy hardware and software exemplifies the importance of considering future data format compatibility during data archiving in the cloud to ensure that archived data remains accessible and usable over time.

213.   D) The significance of maintaining multiple copies of backups in diverse locations

Explanation: The case of the software repository company highlights the significance of maintaining multiple copies of backups in diverse locations to ensure data resilience and availability in the event of a disaster or data loss incident.

214.   A) To irreversibly delete data from storage media

Explanation: The primary objective of cryptographic erasure (crypto shredding) during data destruction in the cloud is to irreversibly delete data from storage media, ensuring that the data cannot be recovered or reconstructed.

215.   A) File storage offers a hierarchical structure, while block storage is unstructured.

Explanation: File storage typically offers a hierarchical structure where files are organized into directories and subdirectories, while block storage is unstructured, consisting of raw blocks of data without any inherent organization.

216.   B) By enhancing data availability

Explanation: Erasure coding enhances availability and improves data resilience in cloud storage architectures. It achieves this by breaking data into fragments, adding redundancy, and distributing these fragments across different storage nodes, allowing for reconstruction in case of node failures.

217.   C) Data loss or theft

Explanation: The risk associated with using highly portable storage media in cloud volume storage architectures is data loss or theft. These storage media can be easily removed or stolen, potentially compromising or losing sensitive data.

218.   C) Performing background checks on provider staff

Explanation: Organizations should consider performing background checks on provider staff when outsourcing data storage to third-party cloud providers to ensure the trustworthiness and integrity of the individuals handling their data.

219.   C) By safeguarding data confidentiality

Explanation: Implementing data encryption in cloud storage contributes to regulatory compliance by safeguarding data confidentiality. Encryption ensures that even if unauthorized parties access data, it remains unreadable and protected, meeting regulatory data privacy and security requirements.

220.   B) The importance of storing cloud backups separately from production data

Explanation: The lesson learned from the case of the software repository company regarding cloud data backup strategies is the importance of storing cloud backups separately from production data to ensure data resilience and availability in the event of a disaster or data loss incident.

221.   A) Objects include metadata and a unique identifier

Explanation: Object storage differs from traditional file or block storage as objects include metadata and a unique identifier, allowing for easier data management and retrieval.

222.   A) PaaS

Explanation: Object storage architectures are most commonly associated with the Platform as a Service (PaaS) cloud service model, where developers can build, deploy, and manage applications without worrying about the underlying infrastructure.

223.   C) To process encrypted data without decryption

Explanation: The primary purpose of homomorphic encryption in cloud computing is to process encrypted data without decryption, allowing for secure computation and analysis of sensitive information while preserving confidentiality.

224.   D) Compression

Explanation: Compression is not typically used for obscuring data in the cloud. Instead, compression reduces data size for efficient storage and transmission.

225.   C) To centralize the collection and analysis of log data

Explanation: The primary purpose of a Security Information and Event Management (SIEM) system is to centralize the collection and analysis of log data from various sources to identify and respond to security incidents and threats.

226.   B) Metadata and unique identifiers

Explanation: Object storage architectures emphasize metadata and unique identifiers, allowing for efficient data management, organization, and retrieval based on metadata attributes.

Answers

227.   B) PaaS

Explanation: Databases are most commonly implemented in the Platform as a Service (PaaS) cloud service model, where providers offer database management systems, allowing users to develop, deploy, and manage databases without managing the underlying infrastructure.

228.   C) Faster data delivery to users

Explanation: The primary advantage of using a Content Delivery Network (CDN) is to improve the speed and efficiency of delivering content to users by caching content closer to them.

229.   D) Encryption in transit

Explanation: Encryption in transit is the process of encrypting data while it is being transmitted over a network, ensuring that it remains secure and private during transmission.

230.   D) Securing encryption keys at the same level as the protected data

Explanation: Key management in cloud computing involves securely managing encryption keys, including storing them separately from the data but with comparable security measures to ensure data remains protected.

231.   C) Enhancing log analysis capabilities

Explanation: The primary goal of Security Information and Event Management (SIEM) implementation is to enhance an organization's ability to analyze logs and detect real-time security incidents.

232.   C) To examine data as it leaves the production environment

Explanation: Egress monitoring in cloud security involves examining data as it leaves the production environment to ensure that sensitive information is not being inappropriately accessed or transmitted.

233.   B) Homomorphic encryption

Explanation: Homomorphic encryption allows for processing encrypted data without decryption, enabling computations to be performed on encrypted data without compromising its security.

234.   B) High processing overhead

Explanation: A critical challenge in implementing Data Loss Prevention (DLP) solutions in cloud environments is the potential for high processing overhead, which can impact system performance.

235.   D) Database as a Service (DaaS)

Explanation: Database as a Service (DaaS) is best suited for implementing databases in cloud environments as it provides a fully managed database service, allowing users to access and utilize databases without the need to manage the underlying infrastructure.

236.   C) Data availability

Explanation: A Content Delivery Network (CDN) primarily aims to improve data availability by distributing content across multiple servers and locations, ensuring it is readily accessible to users.

237.   C) Securing encryption keys at the same level as protected data
Explanation: Critical management in cloud security involves ensuring that encryption keys are secured at the same level as the protected data to prevent unauthorized access.

238.   B) It allows processing of encrypted data without decryption
Explanation: Homomorphic encryption enables computations to be performed on encrypted data without the need for decryption, enhancing privacy and security.

239.   B) Enhanced log analysis capabilities
Explanation: The primary advantage of using a Security Information and Event Management (SIEM) system is its enhanced capability to analyze logs for security events and threats.

240.   D) Compression
Explanation: Compression is not typically used for obscuring sensitive data in cloud environments; instead, it is used for reducing the size of data for storage or transmission.

241.   C) Object storage
Explanation: Object storage architecture is primarily associated with storing data as objects, which include the data itself, along with metadata and a unique identifier.

242.   B) Platform as a Service (PaaS)
Explanation: Databases are most commonly configured to work in Platform as a Service (PaaS) cloud service models, where the underlying infrastructure is managed by the provider.

243.   D) Data latency reduction
Explanation: The primary purpose of a Content Delivery Network (CDN) is to reduce data latency by delivering content to users from the nearest server location.

244.   B) Securing encryption keys at the same level as protected data

Explanation: Key management in cloud security involves securely managing encryption keys at the same level as the protected data to ensure confidentiality and integrity.

245.   B) It allows processing of encrypted data without decryption

Explanation: Homomorphic encryption enables computations to be performed on encrypted data without decryption, maintaining data privacy during processing.

246.   D) Real-time network monitoring

Explanation:

A primary advantage of using a Security Information and Event Management (SIEM) system is its capability for real-time network monitoring and threat detection.

247.   A) DRM

Explanation:

Data Loss Prevention (DLP) can be combined with Digital Rights Management (DRM) to enhance data controls and prevent unauthorized access or distribution of sensitive information.

248.   A) ITAR

Explanation:

The U.S. State Department controls on technology exports are known as International Traffic in Arms Regulations (ITAR).

249.   B) EAR

Explanation:

The U.S. Commerce Department controls on technology exports are known as Export Administration Regulations (EAR).

250.   B) Not stored with the cloud provider
Explanation: Cryptographic keys for encrypted data stored in the cloud should not be stored with the cloud provider to maintain control and prevent unauthorized access.

251.   D) Ensure Multi-factor authentication
Explanation: Best practices for key management include ensuring Multi-factor authentication for added security but not key recovery processes.

252.   A) To a level at least as high as the data they can decrypt
Explanation: Cryptographic keys should be secured to a level at least as high as the data they can decrypt to maintain data confidentiality and integrity.

253.   A) Archive location
Explanation: When crafting plans and policies for data archiving, considerations should include the location of the archive, the backup process, the format of the data, and the immediacy of the technology.

254.   D) Create, Archive, Store, Share, Use, Destroy
Explanation: The correct order of the phases of the data life cycle is Create, Archive, Store, Share, Use, and Destroy.

255.   B) CASBs

Explanation: Third-party providers of IAM (Identity and Access Management) functions for the cloud environment are known as Cloud Access Security Brokers (CASBs).

256.   B) File-based storage
Explanation: A cloud storage architecture that manages data in a hierarchy of files is known as file-based storage.

257.   D) CDN
Explanation: A Content Delivery Network (CDN) manages data in caches of copied content close to locations of high demand, improving the delivery speed and efficiency.

258.   A) Cloud Platform and Infrastructure Security
Explanation: The chapter primarily focuses on Cloud Platform and Infrastructure Security, discussing security measures and best practices in the context of cloud computing.

259.   C) Solely with the cloud customer as the data owner
Explanation: The ultimate legal liability for unauthorized data disclosures in cloud computing typically rests with the cloud customer as the data owner.

260.   C) Adverse effects on the cloud customer's clientele faith
Explanation: One potential consequence for the cloud customer in case of an unauthorized data disclosure event is adverse effects on the cloud customer's clientele faith due to breaches of trust and confidence.

261.   B) Private Cloud

Explanation: Private Cloud deployment model provides an organization with the highest level of autonomy and authority as it offers dedicated resources and infrastructure solely for the organization's use.

262.   C) Potential inability to migrate data to another provider
Explanation: One risk associated with vendor lock-in in cloud computing is the potential inability to migrate data to another provider due to proprietary formats or dependencies.

263.   C) The terms outlined in the service contract
Explanation: The division of responsibilities and risks between the cloud provider and the customer in cloud computing is primarily determined by the terms outlined in the service contract.

264.   D) Regulatory non-compliance
Explanation: Regulatory noncompliance is particularly emphasized when discussing risks associated with public cloud deployment due to the complex and varying regulatory requirements across different regions and industries.

265.   C) Shared costs among members of the community
Explanation: A primary advantage of a community cloud deployment model is shared costs among members of the community, allowing for cost efficiencies and resource optimization.

266.   A) Infrastructure as a Service (IaaS)
Explanation: Infrastructure as a Service (IaaS) provides the highest level of control and autonomy for the cloud customer as they have control over virtualized infrastructure resources.

267.   B) Legal repercussions and fines

Explanation: One potential risk associated with regulatory noncompliance in cloud computing is facing legal repercussions and fines imposed by regulatory authorities for failing to adhere to compliance requirements.

268.   C) By considering migration portability during planning
Explanation: Organizations can enhance the portability of their data in cloud computing by considering migration portability during planning, ensuring compatibility and ease of migration between different cloud environments.

269.   B) Private Cloud
Explanation: The private Cloud deployment model is characterized by the organization controlling the entire infrastructure, including hardware, software, and security controls, providing maximum control and autonomy.

270.   C) Difficulty in migrating data to another provider
Explanation: The primary concern for organizations regarding vendor lock-in in cloud computing is the difficulty in migrating data to another provider, which can result in dependency and limited flexibility.

271.   C) It primarily dictates the division of responsibilities and risks
Explanation: The service contract plays a significant role in determining the division of responsibilities and risks between the cloud provider and the customer by outlining specific obligations, liabilities, and terms of service.

272.   C) Community Cloud
Explanation: The community cloud deployment model offers the most benefits regarding resilience to the loss of infrastructure nodes as resources are shared and dispersed among an affinity group, enhancing redundancy and fault tolerance.

273.   B) Legal repercussions and fines
Explanation: A potential consequence of regulatory noncompliance in cloud computing is facing legal repercussions and fines, which can be substantial and damaging to the reputation and finances of the organization.

274.   D) Scalability and flexibility in resource allocation
Explanation: A primary benefit of a public cloud deployment model is scalability and flexibility in resource allocation, allowing organizations to dynamically adjust resources based on demand without the need for extensive infrastructure investments.

275.   A) Infrastructure as a Service (IaaS)
Explanation: Infrastructure as a Service (IaaS) involves the provider managing and maintaining the underlying infrastructure, including hardware, networking, storage, and virtualization resources.

276.   B) Loss of data due to physical damage to infrastructure
Explanation: A risk associated with natural disasters in cloud computing is the loss of data due to physical damage to infrastructure caused by events such as earthquakes, floods, or hurricanes.

277.   B) Decreased data portability
Explanation: A potential consequence of vendor lock-in in cloud computing is decreased data portability, hindering the organization's ability to migrate to alternative providers or environments.

278.   B) Unauthorized access to sensitive information

Explanation: A risk associated with personnel threats in cloud computing is unauthorized access to sensitive information by malicious insiders, which can lead to data breaches and security incidents.

279.   B) Unauthorized disclosure

Explanation: The risk magnified by cloud computing, particularly concerning internal personnel and remote access, is the unauthorized disclosure of sensitive information due to increased accessibility and potential vulnerabilities.

280.   B) Because of regulatory compliance requirements
Explanation: The entire legal liability for breaches of Personally Identifiable Information (PII) cannot be shifted to the cloud provider due to regulatory compliance requirements and legal obligations that remain with the data owner.

281.   B) Loss of competitive advantage
Explanation: Adverse results from breaches in cloud computing that should be addressed in the Business Impact Analysis (BIA) include loss of competitive advantage, reputational damage, financial losses, and legal ramifications.

282.   D) To evaluate the long-term implications of cloud migration
Explanation: The Business Impact Analysis (BIA) must consider vendor lock-in/lock-out risks to evaluate the long-term implications of cloud migration and ensure that the organization maintains flexibility and control over its data and systems.

283.   D) Service level agreements and uptime guarantees

Explanation: Negotiations between the cloud customer and provider regarding Business Continuity/Disaster Recovery (BC/DR) should address aspects such as service level agreements, uptime guarantees, and responsibilities for BC/DR planning and execution, and audit capabilities.

284.   A) On-premises backup, cloud backup, and third-party backup
Explanation: The three general means of using cloud backups for Business Continuity/Disaster Recovery (BC/DR) are on-premises backup, cloud backup, and third-party backup services.

285.   B) Security of the data and systems and ISP costs

Explanation: Factors to consider in negotiations with cloud providers if the organization maintains its own IT enterprise and uses a cloud provider as a backup include security of the data and systems, internet service provider (ISP) costs, service level agreements (SLAs), and legal compliance.

286.   C) Health and human safety
Explanation: The primary concern in all aspects related to security practices, especially during disaster situations, is health and human safety, ensuring the protection and well-being of individuals involved in response and recovery efforts.

287.   B) To identify vulnerabilities in the backup systems
Explanation: Failover testing is necessary for Business Continuity/Disaster Recovery (BC/DR) plans to identify vulnerabilities in the backup systems and ensure their effectiveness in restoring services in the event of a disaster.

288.   C) Annually
Explanation: According to industry guidance, the recommended frequency for Business Continuity/Disaster Recovery (BC/DR) testing is annual,

although some organizations may choose to conduct testing more frequently based on their specific needs and risk profile.

289.   C) Testing Schedule
Explanation: Coordination with the cloud provider before conducting Business Continuity/Disaster Recovery (BC/DR) testing should include establishing a testing schedule that minimizes disruption to services and ensures cooperation and support from the provider.

290.   C) Timeframe for failover after notice
Explanation: The contract between the cloud customer and provider regarding failover and return to normal operations should explicitly detail the timeframe for failover after notice, ensuring clear expectations and swift response in the event of a disaster.

291.   C) Disaster recovery backup
Explanation: Disaster recovery backup might be at little or no additional cost if offered as part of the standard cloud service, as many cloud providers include basic disaster recovery features and capabilities in their service offerings.

292.   C) To identify vulnerabilities in backup systems
Explanation: The purpose of failover testing in Business Continuity/Disaster Recovery (BC/DR) planning is to identify vulnerabilities in backup systems and ensure they can effectively restore services in the event of a disaster.

293.   D) Vendor lock-in
Explanation: The risk highlighted as being magnified by cloud computing is vendor lock-in, which refers to the dependency of an organization on a

particular cloud provider's services and technologies, limiting the ability to switch providers or migrate to alternative solutions.

294.   B) Because of contractual limitations
Explanation: The entire legal liability for breaches of Personally Identifiable Information (PII) cannot be shifted to the cloud provider due to contractual limitations and regulatory requirements that specify the responsibilities and obligations of both parties.

295.   D) Service level agreements and uptime guarantees
Explanation: Negotiations between the cloud customer and provider regarding failover and return to normal operations should explicitly detail aspects such as service level agreements, uptime guarantees, responsibilities for failover procedures, and communication protocols.

296.   A) On-premises backup, cloud backup, and third-party backup
Explanation: On-premises backup involves storing data locally within the organization's infrastructure, providing control but limited scalability. Cloud backup stores data in remote servers, offering scalability and off-site storage but raising security concerns. Third-party backup outsources backup services to specialized providers, offering expertise and advanced options.

297.   B) Security of the data and systems and ISP costs
Explanation: Factors to consider in negotiations with cloud providers if the organization maintains its IT enterprise and uses a cloud provider as a backup include the security of the data and systems, as well as internet service provider (ISP) costs.

298.   D) Portability

Explanation: The term used to describe the general ease and efficiency of moving data from one cloud provider either to another cloud provider or down from the cloud is "Portability."

299.   B) Continual monitoring for anomalous activity
Explanation: Countermeasures for protecting cloud operations against external attackers include continual monitoring for anomalous activity, hardened devices and systems, and regular configuration/change management activities.

300.   B) Use DRM and DLP solutions widely throughout the cloud operation
Explanation: Techniques to enhance the portability of cloud data to minimize the potential of vendor lock-in include avoiding proprietary data formats, ensuring there are no physical limitations to moving, and ensuring favorable contract terms to support portability. Using DRM (Digital Rights Management) and DLP (Data Loss Prevention) solutions widely throughout the cloud operation is not a technique to enhance portability but rather to enhance security and data protection.

301.   A) Remote kill switch
Explanation: A technique used to attenuate risks to the cloud environment, resulting in the loss or theft of a device used for remote access, is a "Remote kill switch."

302.   A) The cloud provider's suppliers
Explanation: Dependencies that must be considered when reviewing the Business Impact Analysis (BIA) after cloud migration include the cloud provider's suppliers, among other factors.

303.   B) Many states have data breach notification laws.

Explanation: When reviewing the BIA after a cloud migration, new factors related to data breach impacts should be considered, including the fact that many states have data breach notification laws.

304.   A) IaaS
Explanation: In Infrastructure as a Service (IaaS), the cloud customer will have the most control of their data and systems, and the cloud provider will have the least amount of responsibility.

305.   C) The cost-benefit analysis the organization conducted when deciding on cloud migration
Explanation: The material for analyzing the possibility of vendor lock-in/lock-out in the Business Impact Analysis (BIA) after cloud migration may already be available from the cost-benefit analysis the organization conducted when deciding on cloud migration.

306.   C) Unfavorable terms
Explanation: A poorly negotiated cloud service contract could result in unfavorable terms, such as restrictive clauses, insufficient service levels, or unclear responsibilities.

307.   D) Escalation of privilege
Explanation: Specific risks in the public cloud that do not exist in the other cloud service models include escalation of privilege, risk of loss/disclosure due to legal seizures, information bleeding, and DoS/DDoS.

308.   C) Redundant ISPs
Explanation: Countermeasures for protecting cloud operations against internal threats include redundant ISPs, separation of duties, least privilege, and mandatory vacation.

309.   C) DLP solutions

Explanation: Countermeasures for protecting cloud operations against internal threats include DLP (Data Loss Prevention) solutions, separation of duties, least privilege, and mandatory vacation.

310.   D) Mandatory vacation

Explanation: Countermeasures for protecting cloud operations against internal threats include mandatory vacation, separation of duties, least privilege, and conflict of interest.

311.   B) Distributed, remote processing, and storage of data

Explanation: Benefits for addressing BC/DR offered by cloud operations include distributed remote processing and storage of data, fast replication, and metered service.

312.   B) Analysis and review of all log data by trained, skilled personnel on the frequent and effective use of cryptographic sanitization tools

Explanation: Methods used to attenuate the harm caused by escalation of privilege include extensive access control and authentication tools and techniques, the use of automated analysis tools, and cryptographic sanitization tools.

313.   A) Type 1

Explanation: The hypervisor malicious attackers would prefer to attack Type 1, which is a bare-metal hypervisor directly installed on the physical hardware.

314.   B) Vendor lock-out

Explanation: The term used to describe the loss of access to data because the cloud provider has ceased operation is "Vendor lock-out."

315.   C) Backdoors

Explanation: Because PaaS implementations are often used for software development, one of the vulnerabilities that should always be kept in mind is the presence of backdoors, which could be exploited by attackers to gain unauthorized access to the system.

316.   C) To examine the roles and responsibilities of cloud customers and providers

Explanation: Chapter 6 primarily focuses on delineating the respective responsibilities of cloud customers and providers in ensuring the security and integrity of data and services in the cloud environment.

317.   B) Limited control over data storage and processing

Explanation: The text suggests that one of the main challenges for cloud customers is the limited control they have over data storage and processing, as these aspects are often managed by the cloud provider.

318.   A) Service Level Agreement

Explanation: SLA stands for Service Level Agreement, which is a contractual agreement between a service provider and a customer, specifying the level of service expected from the provider.

319.   A) Landlord and tenant

Explanation: The text uses the analogy of a landlord and tenant to describe the relationship between a cloud customer and vendor, where the customer leases space and services from the provider.

Answers

VERSAtile Reads

320.   C) Responsibility for protecting client assets
Explanation: The financial investment analogy highlights the responsibility of cloud customers in protecting their assets, similar to how investors protect their investments in financial markets.

321.   B) They are responsible for legal compliance but lack control over security measures.
Explanation: Cloud customers are responsible for ensuring legal compliance regarding data stored in the cloud, but they may lack direct control over security measures implemented by the cloud provider.

322.   C) Rapidly evolving security standards
Explanation: The text suggests that one of the significant challenges in cloud computing is the rapidly evolving nature of security standards, which makes it challenging for organizations to keep up with the latest developments.

323.   B) Lack of physical access to data centers
Explanation: The text describes the lack of physical access to data centers as "unnatural" in cloud computing, highlighting the difference from traditional on-premises infrastructure where physical access is typically available.

324.   C) Reducing costs and increasing productivity
Explanation: The primary focus of cloud customers is on reducing costs and increasing productivity by leveraging cloud services and resources.

325.   A) HIPAA
Explanation: HIPAA (Health Insurance Portability and Accountability Act) is mentioned as applicable to cloud data centers processing medical information, as it sets standards for the protection of sensitive patient data.

326.   A) Securing the entire infrastructure
Explanation: In an Infrastructure as a Service (IaaS) model, the primary responsibility of the cloud provider is to secure the entire infrastructure, including physical servers, networking components, and virtualization layers.

327.   A) It contains valuable data to attract attackers.
Explanation: A honeypot in cloud security is designed to attract attackers by simulating a vulnerable system or network, allowing security professionals to monitor and analyze their activities.

328.   C) To prevent unauthorized access
Explanation: The primary purpose of a firewall in cloud computing is to prevent unauthorized access to the network and protect against malicious inbound and outbound traffic.

329.   A) By encrypting data in transit
Explanation: Virtual private networks enhance cloud security by encrypting data transmitted between the user's device and the cloud infrastructure, ensuring confidentiality and integrity.

330.   B) Installing and securing applications
Explanation: In a Software as a Service (SaaS) model, the primary responsibility of the cloud customer is to install and secure applications provided by the cloud provider.

331.   C) Managing hardware and software configurations

Explanation: The management plane in cloud data center operations is responsible for managing hardware and software configurations, including provisioning, monitoring, and maintenance activities.

332.　A) A vulnerability assessment focuses on known vulnerabilities, while an IDS detects abnormal behavior.
Explanation: A vulnerability assessment focuses on identifying known vulnerabilities in systems and networks, while an intrusion detection system (IDS) detects abnormal behavior or potential security threats.

333.　D) Exposure to natural disasters
Explanation: When selecting the location of a data center, cloud providers must consider the risk of exposure to natural disasters such as floods, earthquakes, or hurricanes, which could disrupt operations.

334.　A) By implementing strong authentication measures
Explanation: Cloud providers ensure secure remote administrative access to hardware by implementing strong authentication measures, such as multi-factor authentication or certificate-based authentication.

335.　D) To protect against malicious attacks on the hypervisor
Explanation: Configuring hardware components with secure BIOS settings helps protect against malicious attacks on the hypervisor, ensuring the integrity and security of virtualized environments.

336.　B) Configuring virtualized environments
Explanation: In a Platform as a Service (PaaS) model, the cloud provider is responsible for configuring virtualized environments, providing a platform for customers to deploy and manage applications.

337.   C) By controlling access to the facility

Explanation: Cloud providers manage the physical plant of a data center by controlling access to the facility through physical security measures such as access controls, surveillance systems, and security personnel.

338.   A) Configuring virtualized environments

Explanation: Securing Infrastructure as a Service (IaaS) involves shared responsibility between cloud customers and providers, where the provider is responsible for configuring virtualized environments, while the customer is responsible for securing their applications and data within that environment.

339.   B) To explore the challenges of application design and architecture for the cloud.

Explanation: This option aligns with the typical focus of a chapter on cloud application security, which involves understanding the unique challenges posed by designing and architecting applications for cloud environments.

340.   A) Domain 1: Architectural Concepts and Design Requirements.

Explanation: This domain typically encompasses understanding security concepts and requirements within the broader context of cloud architecture and design.

341.   B) Evaluating sensitivity characteristics of data.

Explanation: Understanding the sensitivity of data helps in determining appropriate security measures and compliance requirements before migrating applications to the cloud.

342.   B) Shared responsibility between provider and customer.

Explanation: Cloud service providers and customers typically share responsibility for data security, with the customer having ultimate ownership of the data.

343. C) Forklifting.
Explanation: Forklifting refers to the process of moving an existing application to the cloud with minimal or no modifications to its code.

344. C) Higher susceptibility to tampering.
Explanation: Open-source libraries may have a higher susceptibility to tampering if not carefully managed, potentially leading to security vulnerabilities in cloud applications.

345. A) Lack of available documentation.
Explanation: Developers often face challenges due to the absence or inadequacy of documentation when working in new cloud environments, hindering their ability to understand and navigate the infrastructure.

346. A) Cloud Security Alliance (CSA).
Explanation: The CSA publishes reports such as "The Treacherous 12," which highlight top threats in cloud computing.

347. C) Multitenancy and resource sharing.
Explanation: Multitenancy and resource sharing in cloud environments introduce complexities related to security, resource management, and isolation between tenants.

348. A) Defining.

Explanation: The defining phase of the Cloud Secure Software Development Life Cycle (SDLC) involves identifying business requirements and objectives for the application.

349.   B) Ensuring data security.
Explanation: During the disposal phase, ensuring data security is crucial to prevent unauthorized access or leakage of sensitive information.

350.   B) ISO/IEC 27034-1.
Explanation: ISO/IEC 27034-1 provides guidelines for secure application development practices.

351.   B) Managing user credentials and permissions.
Explanation: IAM primarily focuses on managing user identities, their authentication, and authorization to access cloud resources.

352.   B) Authentication.
Explanation: Authentication is responsible for verifying the identity of users attempting to access cloud resources.

353.   D) Performance degradation due to remote calls.
Explanation: On-premise applications may experience performance issues when deployed in the cloud due to increased network latency and reliance on remote resources.

354.   B) Implementing role-based access controls.
Explanation: Role-based access controls are crucial for controlling user access to cloud resources based on their roles and responsibilities within an organization.

355. B) Facilitating information exchange between organizations.
Explanation: Federation enables seamless and secure information exchange between different organizations' identity management systems.

356. B) Designing.
Explanation: The designing phase of the Cloud Secure SDLC involves developing user stories, interface designs, and architectural plans for the application.

357. C) To control user access to resources.
Explanation: Access management in cloud computing aims to control and regulate user access to cloud resources to maintain security and compliance.

358. B) By publishing reports on cloud computing threats.
Explanation: The Cloud Security Alliance contributes to cloud computing security by publishing reports and guidelines on various threats and best practices.

359. B) Authorization.
Explanation: Authorization is responsible for enforcing access control policies based on predefined rules and business requirements.

360. A) Inclusion of disposal phase.
Explanation: Unlike traditional SDLC, the Cloud-Secure SDLC includes a disposal phase to ensure secure decommissioning of applications and data.

361. B) Incompatibility with cloud infrastructure.

Explanation: Migrating on-premise applications to the cloud may face challenges related to compatibility with the cloud infrastructure and services.

362. C) To highlight top cloud computing threats.
Explanation: The Treacherous 12 report aims to identify and highlight the top threats and risks associated with cloud computing environments.

363. D) Testing.
Explanation: The testing phase of the Cloud Secure SDLC involves conducting vulnerability scanning and penetration testing to identify and mitigate security vulnerabilities.

364. C) To define best practices for software development.
Explanation: ISO/IEC 27034-1 standards aim to define best practices for secure software development processes.

365. B) Authorization.
Explanation: Authorization manages user roles and permissions, determining what actions users are allowed to perform within the cloud environment.

366. B) Validating the trustworthiness of APIs.
Explanation: Validating the trustworthiness of APIs is crucial to ensure the security and reliability of cloud applications relying on them.

367. C) Reduced scalability.
Explanation: Poor documentation can hinder scalability by impeding developers' ability to understand and modify the application as needed for growth.

368.   A) Authentication.

Explanation: Authentication verifies the identity of users and devices attempting to access cloud resources.

369.   A) Independence

Explanation: Independence is the superior benefit of external audit. External audits are often more independent and therefore lead to more effective results.

370.   C) SOX

Explanation: SOX was passed primarily to address the issues of fraudulent accounting practices, poor audit practices, inadequate financial controls, and poor oversight by governing boards of directors.

371. A) SAS 70

Explanation: Before SOX, the AICPA audit standard for reviewing publicly traded corporations was called the SAS 70. SOX mandated a high number of new components for audits, so the AICPA created a new standard that superseded the SAS 70, and that standard is SSAE 16.

372.   A) SOC 1

Explanation: SOC 1 reports a focus on auditing the financial reporting instruments of a corporation.

373.   D) Seal of approval

Explanation: The SOC 3 is the seal of approval. It contains no actual data concerning the security controls of the audit target and is instead just an assertion that the audit was conducted and that the target organization passed.

374. A) To begin the benchmarking process

Explanation: The objective of gap analysis is to start the benchmarking process against risk and security standards and frameworks.

375. D) AICPA

Explanation: Generally Accepted Accounting Practices (GAAP) are created and maintained by the AICPA, which auditors and accountants adhere to in their professions.

376. A) GLBA

Explanation: GLBA provides a superior provision for specifying the many types of protection and controls that financial institutions are necessary to use for securing customers' account information.

377. C) Wholesale or distribution

Explanation: Highly regulated industries such as banking, law enforcement, high-level government agencies, etc. Therefore, wholesale and distribution is not an example of a highly regulated environment.

378. B) Type I

Explanation: A SOC Type I report addresses a specific point in time as opposed to a report of effectiveness over a period.

379. D) Type II

Explanation: A SOC Type II report addresses a specific period as opposed to a specific point in time.

380.   A) The right to no longer pay taxes

Explanation: The right to be forgotten principle specify any individual can notify any entity that has PII for that individual and instruct that entity to delete and destroy all of that individual's PII in that entity's control.

381. A) SLA

Explanation: The right to audit has to be contained in the client's Service-Level Agreement (SLA).

382.   D) All of the above

Explanation: SOX enacted fraudulent accounting practices, poor audit practices, inadequate financial controls, and poor oversight by governing boards of directors.

383.   C) The information security program

Explanation: The essential component of GLBA was the creation of a formal information security program.

384.   D) Financial controls

Explanation: HIPPA does not specify financial controls.

385.   A) How jurisdictional disputes are settled

Explanation: The Doctrine of the Proper Law is a term used to describe the processes associated with determining what legal jurisdiction will hear a dispute when one occurs.

386. A) The basis for deciding which laws are most appropriate in a situation where conflicting laws exist

Explanation: The Restatement (Second) Conflict of Law is a collation of developments in common law that assist the courts in staying up with changes. Numerous states have conflicting laws, and judges use these restatements to help them determine which laws have to be applied when conflicts occur.

387. D) All of the above

Explanation: The Stored Communication Act passed in 1995, is an older law, in bad need of updating, and unclear about newer technologies.

388. B) Self-assessment

Explanation: The lowest level is Level 1, which is self-assessment.

389. B) KRI

Explanation: Key Risk Indicators (KRI) are those items that will be the first things that let you know something is amiss. It might be the announcement of the discovery of a new vulnerability that could affect your cloud provider. The purpose is that you must identify and closely monitor the things that will most quickly alert you to a change in the risk environment.

390. A) ISO 31000:2009

Explanation: ISO 31000:2009 is an international standard that focuses on designing, implementing, and reviewing risk management processes and practices.

391. C) ENISA

Explanation: ENISA identifies the top eight security risks based on likelihood and impact:

- Loss of governance
- Lock-in
- Isolation failure
- Compliance risk
- Management interface failure
- Data protection
- Malicious insider
- Insecure or incomplete data deletion

392. A) Self-assessment, C) SOC 2 audit certification, and D) Continuous monitoring-based certification

Explanation: The CSA STAR program also consists of three levels based on the Open Certification Framework:

- Self-assessment
- Third-party assessment-based certification
- Continuous monitoring–based certification

393. B) ISO/IEC 28000:2007

Explanation: ISO 28000:2007 defines a set of security management requirements, including those that need to be applied to all parties within a supply chain.

394.   A) NIST SP 800-37 and B) European Union Agency for Network and Information Security (ENISA)

Explanation: There are many risk management frameworks that are designed to help the organization in developing sound risk management practices and management. Some of the common risk management frameworks are:

- NIST 800-37
- European Union Agency for Network and Information Security (ENISA)

395.   D) Threat coupled with a vulnerability

Explanation: A threat coupled with a vulnerability is the best definition of a risk.

396.   D) Availability

Explanation: ENISA identifies the top eight security risks based on likelihood and impact:

- Loss of governance
- Lock-in
- Isolation failure
- Compliance risk
- Management interface failure
- Data protection
- Malicious insider
- Insecure or incomplete data deletion

397.   D) Avoidance

Explanation: Avoidance is not a method for handling risk; it means leaving a business opportunity because the risk is simply too high and cannot be compensated for with sufficient control mechanisms.

398.   B) The intermediary who provides connectivity and transport of cloud service between cloud providers and cloud consumers

Explanation: Cloud carriers are the intermediary that provides connectivity and transport of the ISPs between the cloud customer and the cloud provider.

399.   A) Transference

Explanation: Transference is associated with insurance because of the following reason:

The organization pays someone else to accept the risk, at a lower cost than the potential impact that would result from the risk being realized; this is usually in the form of insurance.

400.   C) Use of subcontractors

Explanation: The use of subcontractors can add risk to the supply chain and has to be considered; trusting the provider's management of their vendors and suppliers (including subcontractors) is significant to trusting the provider.

About Our Products

Other products from VERSAtile Reads are:

 Elevate Your Leadership: The 10 Must-Have Skills

 Elevate Your Leadership: 8 Effective Communication Skills

 Elevate Your Leadership: 10 Leadership Styles for Every Situation

 300+ PMP Practice Questions Aligned with PMBOK 7, Agile Methods, and Key Process Groups – 2024

 Exam-Cram Essentials Last-Minute Guide to Ace the PMP Exam - Your Express Guide featuring PMBOK® Guide

 Career Mastery Blueprint - Strategies for Success in Work and Business

 Memory Magic: Unraveling the Secret of Mind Mastery

 The Success Equation Psychological Foundations For Accomplishment

 Fairy Dust Chronicles – The Short and Sweet of Wonder

 B2B Breakthrough – Proven Strategies from Real-World Case Studies

VERSAtile Reads

 CISSP Fast Track Master: CISSP Essentials for Exam Success

 CISA Fast Track Master: CISA Essentials for Exam Success

 CISM Fast Track Master: CISM Essentials for Exam Success

www.ingramcontent.com/pod-product-compliance
Lightning Source LLC
LaVergne TN
LVHW081341050326
832903LV00024B/1254